JOHN LUCAS

Low-Water Gardening

J. M. DENT
London

Published in
association with
the Council for
the Protection of Rural England

First published 1993

British Library Cataloguing-in-Publication Data
A catalogue record for this book is available from
The British Library
ISBN 0 460 86117 4 (hardback)
ISBN 0 460 86151 4 (paperback)

Typeset by Selwood Systems, Midsomer Norton
Printed and bound in Great Britain by
Butler & Tanner Ltd, Frome and London for
J. M. Dent Ltd
The Orion Publishing Group
Orion House
5 Upper St Martin's Lane
London WC2H 9EA

Low-Water Gardening

John Lucas, who first trained as a
draughtsman, environmental designer and
technical author, is a landscape and garden
design consultant. He writes and lectures
on garden design and horticultural subjects
and is a specialist lecturer for both the
Inchbald School of Design and the College
of Garden Design, as well as being principal
lecturer on the Advanced Garden Design
course for the London Open College
Federation. He is a member of the Society
of Garden Designers and principal design
consultant of his landscape and design
practice, John H. Lucas & Associates, at
West Ewell in Surrey.

Contents

Photographs

Line Illustrations

Introduction

The aim of this book is to take a look at common gardening practices in the new light of the lack of water resources. It revises and updates old, tried and tested gardening procedures to make them applicable to today's climatic conditions. In particular it highlights, and provides a step-by-step guide to avoiding, the irrigation inefficiencies of many current horticultural practices. Whilst the book therefore concentrates on the practical aspects of gardening without wasting water, and includes a comprehensive list of plants and trees that will thrive under drought conditions, it also contains a great deal of information on the theory and practice of good design, which is an essential aspect of successful gardening.

Over the last decade, gardening has become an ever more popular pastime and millions of pounds are now spent each year in developing, constructing and maintaining the garden around our homes. The presence of a garden centre in almost every town means that the purchase of plants, trees and garden sundries is within easy reach of everyone, and a visit to a garden centre any weekend in spring or summer will contend to their popularity. I well remember a time when bare-rooted trees and shrubs, with their roots wrapped in hessian, could only be safely planted in the dormant season. Now, because of container planting, the variety of plants and trees available to the gardener at all times of the year is vast.

Whilst selecting plants can be an exciting adventure to those who are experienced and knowledgeable in the subject, to others it can present great problems. Most garden centres do their best to enlighten the general public by detailed plant labels and catalogues, but these can only provide limited information. It is a sad fact that many plants are purchased on a whim. Because of a fine display of foliage or flower, many plants are bought without any thought for the growing conditions they will require. Often, very little consideration is given to soil type, aspect, hardiness, habit, rate of growth, ultimate size and resistance to disease. The result is often a plant that requires constant nurture and feeding, which would not have been necessary if the right growing conditions had existed in the first place. A fine example is the addition of peat to neutral or slightly alkaline soil in order to grow healthy acid-loving plants such as rhododendron or azaleas. This was an accepted practice for many years and has played a major part in the overworking of the peat reserves.

Over the last few years a new problem has arisen which has had to be taken into account when purchasing and maintaining plants: the lack of water for irrigation. Once, the addition onto the household water bill of the use of a hose secured all the water anyone could wish for. A sprinkler working all evening over a shrub or herbaceous border was a common sight. Sadly, those days are now gone and some areas of the country are under constant threat of a hosepipe ban. This restriction has caused anger and frustration amongst gardeners, many of whom have ignored the ban, with some incurring the resultant fine.

Whilst I fully understand the gardener's anger at being denied the use of water during a drought, the time is now upon us when we can no longer ignore the problem of water shortage. The reduction of ground water reserves has increased over the last few years to such an extent that it is fast becoming a national crisis. Some of the statistics are very sobering. Public demand for water has increased by 70 per cent over the last thirty years. This rise occurs in the use of water for domestic purposes such as garden watering and car washing and is mainly due to ever more development in the south and east of England. Because of the loss of heavy industry in the north and midlands, water previously stored for use in such areas is now in the wrong place.

The problem in the south and east of England is made worse by the reduction of ground water supplies due to low rainfall and exceptionally dry summers over recent years. As 40–70 per cent of the water supply for these areas is dependent on the ground water reserves, the authorities are faced with a severe problem of supply and demand.

To understand the problem fully, it is useful to know a little about how the ground water reserves are held and replenished. When rain falls, some is immediately evaporated into the atmosphere, whilst some percolates into the soil to become subsurface water. Some of this subsurface water is taken up by plants and trees and is then transpired into the atmosphere through their leaves. The remainder passes down, under the influence of gravity, into water-bearing rock called an aquifer, which is the source of all our ground water supply. The upper surface of this area of water is known as the water table and over recent years this level has fallen considerably in many areas.

The result of a lowering of the water table can be seen in the drying up of many streams and water courses and the change of areas from wetland to rough grazing. Some of the most beautiful rivers of Great Britain are being transformed from delightful habitats where wildlife once thrived to rubbish dumps devoid of any aquatic plants or wildlife. Although the loss of such rivers evokes strong emotions in local residents, it is only recently that their distress has become known to the general public. Whilst there are those who will nod wisely and say that nature will redress the balance in due course, it is increasingly likely that global warming may cause rainfall patterns in the future to become extremely erratic. It is now becoming obvious, even to the layman, that our whole outlook on the supply of water will require radical change.

The effects on horticulture and agriculture are already being felt with the restriction on irrigation. However, it is my contention that more far-reaching steps must be considered, including giving much greater thought to the selection of the plants and trees we include in our gardens and open spaces. How often does the plant label at our garden centre mention how the plant thrives under conditions of drought? Many of the plants and trees with which we fill our parks and gardens at present are totally unsuitable for drought conditions. Under a regime where irrigation is a major problem, the right selection of plants and trees to suit such conditions will become a major part of gardening.

CHAPTER ONE

Preparing the Garden for Drought Conditions

This was one of my prayers: for a parcel of land not so very large, which should have a garden and spring of ever-flowing water near the house, and a bit of woodland as well as these.

Horace, 65–8 BC

In the past, when water was available on demand, the need to design and plant our gardens for drought conditions was not considered important. However, with the change of climate over recent years and the drastic reduction in water reserves, such a need has now become one of the most vital factors. Present water supply levels demand that we give more thought to the water-retentive properties of our soils. The purpose of this chapter is to illustrate the ways in which we may plan our gardens in order to make the best use of any water available.

UNDERSTANDING OUR SOIL

If we pick up some soil from our garden, we have in our hand a part of the life force on which all plants and trees depend. Soil is the major source of all our food and is closely linked with the history of mankind. Until the Industrial Revolution, our whole economy was based on the soil and man was an integral part of the growing process. Today, the majority of people living in our highly technical world have lost this link with the soil. However, with a little understanding, the development and conditioning

of the soil in the gardens surrounding our homes can be extremely rewarding.

In a normal, good, garden soil, the bulk will consist of mineral fragments
which have resulted from the breakdown of igneous, sedimentary or meta-
morphic rock. This mineral element has no ability to make plants grow;
it is only by the addition of organic matter, produced by the decomposition
of plant and animal life, that soil is able to provide the required conditions
for growth. In addition to minerals and organic matter, good soil must also
contain soil air, which is trapped in the larger pores between the soil
particles; soil water, which is held in minute spaces within the soil structure, and a population of living organisms to break down the organic
matter. For any soil to act as a good growing medium it must therefore
have the correct balance of mineral and organic matter; its structure must
be able to retain the correct amount of soil air and water, and it must
encourage the growth of living micro-organisms.

Soil Testing

Everyone who is developing or planting a garden should first get to know
the type and condition of their soil. Lack of such knowledge can often
result in disappointment when initially healthy plants become sick and
carefully thought-out planting schemes fail. For the sake of a few pounds
and a little time, many fine plants could be saved from dying by either
selecting more suitable plants, which will thrive in the existing soil, or by
modifying the texture of the soil to suit the required plants.

Whilst it is possible to send off samples of soil to a laboratory and obtain
a detailed analysis of their complete chemical make-up, all the garden
owner generally requires to know is whether the soil is acid or alkaline
and what texture it has. There are some instances where a more detailed
analysis is advantageous, such as on landfills or where the land has been
used previously for industrial or commercial purposes. However, if the
land has not been affected by the harmful chemicals that may be present
in landfills and industrial sites, testing for acidity/alkalinity is usually
sufficient.

Testing for pH

Soil acidity/alkalinity is measured in pH and knowledge of a garden soil's pH value is vital in determining which plants will thrive and which will fail. Often one is able to make a judgement on the soil simply by noting the types of plants that grow well in it. For example, rhododendron and azaleas flourish in acid soils, whilst daphne and buddleia thrive in alkaline soils where the rhododendron would suffer badly. However, in order to make a more accurate assessment it will be necessary to purchase or borrow a pH test kit. There are two types of such kit on the market, the chemical kit and the probe. Both are moderately priced and are well worth owning.

The method of testing with the chemical kit is to select samples of soil from various parts of the garden. The location of each sample should be recorded and each should be tested separately. The sample is placed in the phial provided and the supplied liquid added to a given level. With the end of the phial plugged, the mixture is then shaken and left until it has finished changing colour. The final colour is then checked against a chart and the acidity value read off in pH. If an accurate reading is to be obtained, it is imperative that the liquid and phial are kept clean throughout: even blocking the end of the phial with the thumb will affect the accuracy of the test.

The probe is much easier to use as it is simply inserted into moist soil and the pH level read from the display. Although the probe therefore has the advantage of simplicity and may be used time and time again, the results can be less accurate if great care is not taken. It is possible, for example, to obtain an incorrect reading if the probe is not inserted into the soil properly and does not make satisfactory contact. Care must also be taken to avoid the probe being damaged by careless handling, as once damaged it cannot be repaired.

The result of both the above methods will be a set of figures representing the tests of various parts of the garden. If there are any vast discrepancies between sets of figures, the respective areas should be retested for accuracy.

The resultant figures may now be checked against a pH scale. The theoretical pH scale ranges from 0, which is extremely acid, to 14, which is extremely alkaline. Thus a pH of 7 is considered neutral. However, in practice, the pH of a soil will rarely extend below 3.5 even in a peat bog, or above 8.5, in very chalky soils.

The pH figures obtained in the tests will establish which plants will grow well in your garden soil and which will suffer. It is not good practice to attempt to alter the acidity of soil in large quantities as this is both expensive and inefficient. There is a wonderful selection of plants both for acid and alkaline conditions and if you have a neutral soil, the choice is vast.

Testing Soil Texture

The texture of your soil will greatly affect growing conditions, especially in times of drought, and it is imperative to establish which type of soil you have.

Sand Soils
Sandy soils drain very quickly, with the subsequent loss of valuable nutrients. They are nearly always very acid and dry out very quickly. Because sandy soils warm up quickly they may be cultivated much earlier in the season than clay-based soils.

Silt Soils
Silt is generally very acid and has very fine particles which pack together when wet. When dry, it is difficult to control and will tend to blow away in windy conditions. Untreated silt soils are very difficult to work. Often, many 'silt soils' are mixtures of fine sand and clay, which are much more fertile and easier to work than true silt soils.

Clay Soils
Clay soils are usually rich in nutrients but are hard to drain and very slow to warm up. Untreated, they are very difficult and heavy to work. However, if treated properly, clay-based soils offer very good growing conditions due to their ability to hold nutrients in the pore structure.

Loam
Loam is the name given to a well-balanced soil containing the right ratio of sand, silt, clay and micro-organisms. Loam offers excellent growing conditions, is fairly quick to warm up, but offers good drainage. If there is a preponderance of sand, then it is known as a sandy loam; if a preponderance of clay, it is known as a clay loam.

The Thumb and Finger Test

It is possible to make a fairly accurate test of the type of soil you have in your garden by conducting a thumb and finger test. Wet a sample of soil about the size of a walnut and work it to break down all crumbs until it is smooth. Rub the sample between your thumb and fingers and assess as follows:

If the soil feels gritty and will not form a ball when rolled in the hand, then it is *sandy*.

If the soil does not feel gritty but feels soapy and silky, then it is *silty*.

If the soil sticks slightly to the fingers and is slightly plastic, it is a *loam*.

If the soil forms a ball when rolled in the hand but still feels slightly sandy and does not stick to the fingers, it is a *sandy loam*.

If the soil is slightly sandy and is very sticky and plastic, it is a *sandy clay*.

If the soil is very sticky and forms a glaze when rubbed, it is *clay*.

If the soil is sticky but does not glaze when rubbed, it is a *clay loam*.

SOIL CONDITIONING

As may be seen from the above, the best soil type for growing most plants is a neutral loam, rich in both organic matter and micro-organisms. For each person who finds themselves the fortunate owner of such a garden there must be thousands who take over a piece of land which has certain soil deficiencies. In such cases it will be necessary to condition or treat the soil to improve its structure and increase its capacity for encouraging micro-organisms. Where soils are acid, I would not suggest that any attempt is made to change the pH drastically as this is often unsatisfactory. Instead, it is far better to establish the pH of your soil and purchase plants that will grow well in it. If one really wants to grow acid-loving plants in an alkaline soil, it is far better to grow them in raised beds or containers, where special, ericaceous soil can be easily maintained.

Improving Sandy Soils

As sandy soils warm up quickly they are good for producing early crops of vegetables and are usually suitable for acid-loving plants with long root systems which can search out water from deep in the ground. However, sandy soils will not retain moisture, which will cause great problems in drought conditions. The old method for improving sandy soil was to incorporate clay in large quantities. This was known as 'marling' and was very popular in the eighteenth century. Today, though, because of relatively high transport and labour costs, it is more practical to increase the proportion of organic matter in the soil.

Well-rotted farmyard manure applied at root level will radically increase the water-holding capacity of a previously untreated sandy soil. If you are fortunate to have a ready supply of matured garden compost, this will also greatly improve soil conditions. Other options are available, such as straw, hops, leaf mould and spent mushroom compost, but these are often best composted prior to incorporation in the soil as they may take nitrogen from the soil whilst decomposing.

Any work undertaken in cultivating sandy soil is best left until spring, immediately prior to sowing. This will reduce the loss of nutrients, which may be washed away during winter rainfalls.

Improving Clay Soils

Usually, advice given on the improvement of clay soils revolves around improving drainage, including installing land drains and adding bulk materials such as sand and burnt clay. However, adding sand, gravel or granulated brick, for example, to a clay soil in order to improve drainage will only be effective if a considerable amount is used and will not go far to improve *controlled* water retention, which should be our aim.

Clay soils retain moisture because the soil particles are very fine and soil water is held by capillary attraction between the pores. This soil water is rich in nutrients and must not be lost. Any improvement, therefore, must concentrate on improving the openness of the soil whilst maintaining water retention. This is best done by incorporating organic matter, most of which will decompose. The undecomposed parts, such as roots, leaves and stems, will keep the soil open, providing passages through which air can enter and excess water can pass.

The speed of decomposition of organic matter, into a black or brown material known as humus, depends on the condition of the soil. In a healthy, rich soil in which earthworms and micro-organisms are present, organic matter is broken down much more quickly than in poor, badly drained soil. Thus, in a poorly worked clay soil, decomposition may take some time. However, the presence of humus will make the soil more open, thus improving both aeration and drainage. As the humus is continually lost to the soil it must be replaced in the form of well-rotted farmyard manure, garden compost, straw, hops, or leaf mould.

It is important to avoid working clay soils when they are very wet as this will destroy their structure and cause compaction. The best time to carry out digging is in the autumn, when the soil is fairly dry, leaving it in large lumps for the frost to break down during the winter.

Improving Silt Soils

The general method for improving silt soils is similar to that for sandy soils and centres on the addition of organic matter. However, silt particles are so fine that they will pack together when wet to form a hard crust on the surface of the soil (known as capping) through which rainwater cannot penetrate. It is therefore important that the surface of the soil is kept open by hoeing, which will break up any compaction.

Adding Organic Matter to the Soil

As the inclusion of organic matter in the soil is a priority when improving its water-retentive properties, it is worth considering some practical methods of adding compost such as farmyard manure.

Where a new area of land is to be developed as a garden, it is relatively simple to work in organic matter. The area should be cleared of all perennial weeds and large stones and then double dug. Organic matter should be added at both levels of digging so that it will be evenly distributed. The best time to undertake this work is in the autumn, which will allow the winter frosts to break down any large lumps of soil. This is especially useful in clay-based soils.

Adding organic matter to an already established bed or border is more difficult but not impossible if one employs the energies of the earthworm. Although it is possible to dig in fairly large quantities of organic matter between large shrubs, care must be taken not to damage the root system. By creating a soil environment in which the earthworm will thrive, much of the organic material placed on, or near, the surface of the soil will be taken down to root level. Therefore, the best method is to work as much organic matter as possible into the top soil and then apply a 10cm mulch of well-rotted compost over the whole area. If there is a supply of earthworms, say from a compost bin or wormary, that can be added with the organic material, then the whole process can be speeded up. It is best if any organic matter added to the soil is fresh, moist and rich. Compost or farmyard manure that has been lying around in the sun for days will take a considerable time to settle into the soil before earthworms will be encouraged to inhabit it. As earthworms work better in warm soil conditions, the above treatment for established beds and borders is best undertaken in the spring.

SUPPLYING ADDITIONAL NUTRIENTS

If bulk organic material is added to the soil in the form of farmyard manure or compost it will provide much of the nutrients required by the plants for healthy growth. However, it is sometimes necessary to provide additional nutrients in the form of fertilisers, which act more directly on the plant. It is important that the gardener is aware of the effects such fertilisers have if the proper balance of growth is to be maintained. The three essential fertilisers are nitrogen (N), phosphate (P) and potassium (K). Commercial fertilisers provide a ratio of N:P:K depending on the use for which the fertiliser is required. For example, a balanced fertiliser such as National Growmore is $N7:P7:K7$, that is, nitrogen, phosphate and potassium are each provided at the rate of seven parts per hundred. On the other hand, a popular fertiliser recommended for roses, tomatoes and all flowering plants has an NPK of $N10:P10:K27$, that is, the fertiliser contains the extra potassium required by the plant to form and develop the flowers and fruit.

Although there are many nutrients required for balanced plant growth, I will simply give details of the more important mineral nutrients.

Nitrogen (N)

Nitrogen affects the rate and strength of growth of the plant and provides a healthy leaf colour. Thus, a plant that shows signs of yellowing may be suffering from a nitrogen deficiency. Such a deficiency is a common problem in new ground where raw organic matter has been added, because the nitrogen is being taken from the soil as the organic matter decomposes. In such a case, the lost nitrogen should be replaced in the form of either ammonium nitrate, ammonium sulphate, calcium nitrate, potassium nitrate, dried blood or hoof and horn in the quantities indicated by the supplier. Great care must be taken not to overdose with nitrogen as that will produce soft growth, which is vulnerable to pest attack; it may also produce high salt concentrates within the plant roots. Furthermore, when nitrogen is added to the soil it must be accompanied by a supply of potassium or a deficiency in the latter will arise.

Other signs that soil is lacking in nitrogen are stunted growth and weak stems. However, as there is a trace element, molybdenum, which assists in the uptake of nitrogen, a possible shortage of molybdenum should be considered when treating for nitrogen deficiency.

Phosphorus (P)

Phosphorus is essential for good root growth; it also speeds up the development of flowers, seeds and fruits. As phosphorus has a low solubility it is not easily taken up by the root system and so good soil preparation, including the addition of organic matter, is vital. Furthermore, in order to reduce the need for the root system to search for phosphate within the soil, it is best if a fertiliser rich in phosphate is applied near the roots during planting or major digging. Thus, the addition of a handful of bonemeal to the planting hole for trees and shrubs has become a habit to most gardeners.

Signs of a lack of phosphorus are stunted roots, a general reduction in plant growth, and a marked reduction in the yield of fruit and seeds.

Leaves may also be reduced in size and lose their colour.

Potassium (K)

Potassium, known to the gardener as potash, is necessary for the development of flowers and the correct formation of fruit. As it also improves the plants' general resistance to drought and disease it is an important nutrient when planting with drought conditions in mind. Potassium also assists photosynthesis and the production of carbohydrate. Many sandy soils may be low in potassium as it is easily washed away from soils which are low in organic matter.

Signs of a lack of potassium are a mottling, spotting or curling of leaves, which may also appear scorched at the edges. Where there is a potassium deficiency in fruit trees, the fruits may lose their colour.

Calcium (Ca)

Calcium is vital for the development of young plants and a shortage will reduce the ability of some species of plant to assimilate nitrogen. Lack of calcium will show as a general reduction in the growth and health of the plant.

Magnesium (Mg)

Magnesium is necessary for seed germination and, as it is a part of the chlorophyll molecule, any deficiency will result in loss of leaf colour. It is also a basic requirement for the formation of amino acids and vitamins. Lack of magnesium will be indicated by a general deterioration in the leaves of the plant and, in some instances, premature leaf loss.

Boron (B)

Boron affects various processes within the plant, including the translocation of sugars and the dormancy rate of seed in some plants. A boron deficiency can result in suppressed flowering and the production of malformed fruit.

Sulphur (S) and Iron (Fe)

Both these minerals affect chlorophyll production, so any shortage will be indicated by a loss of leaf colour. With a sulphur deficiency, the leaves may become light green, whereas an iron deficiency my produce chlorosis and weak leaf stems.

Zinc (Zn)

Zinc is important in the healthy formation of seeds and general plant growth, especially the leaves. Lack of zinc will result in misshaped leaves and may cause iron deficiency.

THE USE OF PEAT AND ITS ALTERNATIVES

I have deliberately avoided including peat in the list of water-retentive organic matter with which to treat our soil. Whilst there is little doubt that it is the best organic material for holding water, there is much controversy at present regarding its use in the horticultural industry and as a planting aid in the garden.

On the one hand there are the conservationists, who are concerned at the loss of the peat bogs. They argue that these bogs offer a unique environment which is attractive to birds and wildlife and contains many rare species of plants and insects. Peat bogs also lock in vast quantities of carbon dioxide, which is the source material for the greenhouse effect, and serve as reservoirs for surplus water in wet seasons.

On the other hand, the peat producers argue that there is no shortage of peat in the world. Although 2.7 million cubic metres of peat are used each year for horticultural purposes, a recent report by the Horticultural Development Council states that, of the 1.5 million hectares of peat in the UK, only 8,000 hectares are worked. The report goes on to say that the world reserves of peat at present are some 150 million hectares. It does, however, recognise that peat is not an easily renewable resource and that every effort should be made to find a suitable alternative.

Peat is formed over hundreds of thousands of years by the decomposition of plants in acid wetlands. There are two main types:

Sphagnum Peat

This contains sphagnum mosses. As it provides good water retention, it is the more popular peat for general horticultural use as a propagation and potting medium.

Sedge Peat

This is formed from sedges and reed grasses and is much richer in nutrients than sphagnum peat. Its structure is excellent for making peat blocks for general horticultural use.

Finding Alternatives to Peat

The main problem with finding a renewable alternative is that peat is a unique planting medium. It is a very reliable material, with an excellent air to water ratio, a low pH and a known nutrient content. As it is generally free from all plant and human content, it is safe to work with and, at present, is relatively competitive to produce. Because of these qualities there is currently no truly satisfactory alternative to peat for horticultural use, although many attempts are being made to find one. Any substitute must be environmentally friendly, be renewable and be competitively priced. For the gardener at home, however, who is using relatively small quantities of peat for planting and mulching, there are some substitutes available at garden centres.

As a mulch or soil conditioner, the bark-based composts are quite good. Leaf mould is used widely in the USA as a soil conditioner and Kew Gardens composts 5,000 cubic metres per year for their own use. Animal manure mixed with straw is employed at the moment in agriculture and may be developed for the garden in the future. Composts produced from coconut fibre are becoming more popular and sewage residues may be used more once problems of contamination have been overcome.

For water retention, well-rotted compost is probably still the best substitute for peat and has the bonus of being rich in nutrients. As the nutrient values of peat substitutes vary, it is wise to check any material prior to its purchase. Low-nutrient organic materials are used as bulking materials; high-nutrient organic materials will require diluting with low nutrient materials.

MULCHING

If one turns over a stone or piece of wood lying on the ground, the soil will be damp underneath in anything but the worst drought because the stone or wood has reduced the water evaporation from the surface of the soil. This is one of the main advantages of mulching, which is the covering of the soil surface with a suitable material. In addition to reducing evaporation, a mulch will also suppress weeds, reduce heat loss, erosion and soil compaction and improve crop production.

In general horticultural use, many organic materials are employed as a mulch, including straw, leaf mould, compost, lawn mowings and spent mushroom compost. However, it is important that any mulch, whilst reducing evaporation, does not prevent entry of rainwater.

In the relatively small areas of a private garden it is possible to include more expensive materials, such as granulated forest bark and gravel, in our list of mulches. However, in order to be truly effective, the mulch should be at least 5cm thick and, if funds will allow, preferably 10cm thick.

It is often beneficial to cover the soil with a soil mat such as biddim or teram prior to laying the mulch. This will have the extra advantage of suppressing weeds whilst allowing water to percolate to root level. I have seen black polythene used for this purpose, but I do not find this so satisfactory over long periods because it deteriorates. By cutting slots in the surface of the sheets, planting can then be undertaken and the mulch formed round the plant stems.

CHAPTER TWO

Efficient Irrigation and Storage of Water

When that I was and a little tiny boy, with hey, ho, the wind and the rain. A foolish thing was but a toy, for the rain it raineth every day.
Shakespeare, *The Two Gentlemen of Verona*, I.1.2

When I was a lad, I spent long periods during my school summer holidays on a farm in Sussex owned by my uncle and aunt. The only water available for all household and horticultural uses came from a well, and one of the first things the children of the family were asked to do each morning was to hand-pump water into the main storage tank in the roof of the house. Whilst staying with the family I had to turn my hand to this task and although at first it was something of a novelty, it was also very hard for underdeveloped muscles not used to such work. I can still remember, however, how precious that water was and how I didn't want to see any wasted, even for washing up or what I felt was overuse of the toilet. Now, all the farms and houses in that area of Sussex are connected to the mains water supply and I am sure that very little thought is given to how much water is being used by any members of the household, young or old.

In a very simple way this story reflects the problem of overuse and waste of water. It is all too easy now to turn on a tap and have instant, high quality water for all household and garden uses. However, with the change of climate over recent years and the drastic reduction in water reserves, it is now imperative that we all give thought to the ways in which water is being wasted at present and such waste can be prevented. This is not as difficult as it may seem once the will is there. Those who have had water meters fitted to their mains water supply very soon discover ways of making savings and we can all learn from such experiences. Even stopping what initially appears to be a minor waste, such as leaving the tap running whilst cleaning your teeth or leaving the hose on when cleaning the car, very quickly adds up to considerable savings over a year. Other and much greater savings may be made within the house. For instance, the average bath uses approximately 135 litres of water, whilst a five-minute shower only uses around 65 litres; a saving of 70 litres could be made every time one showers instead of bathing.

The aim of this chapter is to indicate ways in which water may be used efficiently in the garden. It also provides ideas on ways to avoid wasting treated water by the storage of rainwater and water from the house.

In commercial horticulture, irrigation is seen as a part of crop husbandry and often involves the setting up of an irrigation plan, which closely relates the amount of water required by any particular crop to the prevailing soil conditions. However, when considering an irrigation system for the garden of a private home the approach can be totally different.

It is a simple fact that young and newly established plants require regular watering for their roots to develop correctly. Therefore, the purpose of an efficient irrigation system for the private garden should be to provide sufficient water to support the growth of a type of root system that will make the adult plant as self-sufficient as possible in any future drought conditions.

Except for conifers, which benefit from watering through their foliage, most plants take up water and nutrients through their root systems. To be truly efficient, therefore, a watering system should supply water to root level whilst keeping evaporation and seepage to a minimum.

In addition to regular watering when young, it is important that plants are selected, and soil conditions are provided, that will make the plants as self-sufficient as possible in drought conditions. Thus, plants with deep root systems that will reach down into the water table are better suited than shallow-rooting plants.

The addition of organic matter at root level, as previously mentioned, will greatly assist in proper root development. Also, the way that water is supplied to the plants will greatly affect the development of the right type of root system. If water is provided in small quantities at the surface of the soil, the roots will be encouraged to stay shallow in order to absorb such moisture. If, however, as the young plants are developing, water is provided at root level, this will encourage the formation of a good root system.

The use of a hosepipe or sprinkler in the garden, once a very common sight, is very inefficient as it results in high levels of evaporation from the surface of the foliage and soil, especially if the soil is compacted. As the rate of evaporation increases with higher air temperatures, increased wind speed and the lowering of humidity levels, watering with sprays and sprinklers in summer, when water reserves are most at risk, can be particularly wasteful. It is far better to investigate efficient ways of providing water at root level for young plants.

The simplest and least expensive method when planting new trees and shrubs is to sink vertical sections of earthenware drainpipe into the ground so that one end of the pipe is slightly above the plant roots. The pipe should then be filled with very coarse gravel. It is then easy to water into the pipe, either from a can, a hose, or with a fixed-drip watering system controlled by a valve.

It is also possible to purchase, at reasonable cost, a complete drip-irrigation system for the whole garden. Although this type of system can lead to a high percentage of evaporation if the water falls onto the top of the soil, especially if the soil is compacted, it can be much improved by using it in association with the vertical pipe system described above. If one is employing such a system, control is essential if water is not to be wasted. Whether the drip system is fitted to the mains water supply or to a rainwater storage tank, it is all too easy to leave on the tap, with the subsequent waste of water. It is possible to purchase a timer-controlled water valve, which enables a regular watering scheme to be established. Again, this must be monitored as watering requirements will vary with the seasons and weather conditions.

While I feel that, except for planting of conifers, watering via a conventional sprinkler or spray system should be generally avoided, there are times when a foliage spray will help clean leaves of harmful dust, etc., especially if the garden is adjacent to a main road. Any such watering with sprinklers or sprays is best undertaken at dusk, when evaporation will be kept to a minimum.

THE EFFICIENT STORAGE OF WATER

It does not seem so long ago that every house appeared to have at least one rainwater butt for catching the water from roofs. Today such water

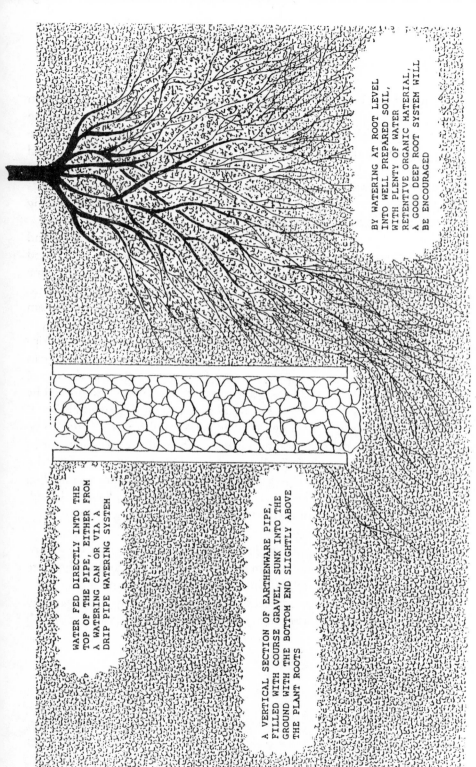

WATER FED DIRECTLY INTO THE
TOP OF THE PIPE, EITHER FROM
A WATERING CAN OR VIA A
DRIP PIPE WATERING SYSTEM

A VERTICAL SECTION OF EARTHENWARE PIPE,
FILLED WITH COURSE GRAVEL, SUNK INTO THE
GROUND WITH THE BOTTOM END SLIGHTLY ABOVE
THE PLANT ROOTS

BY WATERING AT ROOT LEVEL
INTO WELL PREPARED SOIL,
WITH PLENTY OF WATER
RETENTIVE ORGANIC MATERIAL,
A GOOD DEEP ROOT SYSTEM WILL
BE ENCOURAGED

Fig. 1. *Watering system with a vertical pipe*

storage is not such a common sight, which is a pity as it is a highly efficient source of water. If a water container is fitted with a lid to exclude the light, the condition of the water will remain very good for long periods. By fitting a tap to a butt it is a simple matter to fill a watering can or a water barrow, although it is much easier and more efficient if the water butt is connected to a drip-watering system as described above. By connecting a hose from the butt to vertical watering pipes filled with gravel, the water can be easily transferred to where it will do most good, at very little cost and no labour.

The static pressure from a barrel or tank placed directly on the ground (barrels and tanks should always be raised slightly off the ground with a waterproof membrane such as builders' felt placed between the tank and the support) is fairly low and the subsequent hose pressure will also be low when compared with the pressure from a mains water tap. This can be increased by raising the tank off the ground on piers.

The water-collecting potential of a standard, three- or four-bedroom house is astounding. For example, with an average annual rainfall the roof of a semidetached house may collect between 40,000 and 50,000 litres of rain water per annum. Although it would obviously not be possible to keep such a large quantity of water around the house without considerable expenditure on storage facilities, even a small percentage would assist in the efficient watering of new shrubs and trees. The commercial possibilities of such bulk storage are already being explored. It is now possible to purchase a system which will not only store all of the rainwater that falls on the house roof, but the system will also purify and filter the water under ultraviolet light to remove bacteria and viruses. As the cost of such a system is about half the price of a small family car it may not seem very appealing at present. However, when the cost of water begins to increase, such storage systems may become far more attractive.

Even if such expenditure on a bulk water storage system was not considered feasible, it would be possible to store quantities of water of up to 5,000 litres if the will was there. For instance, there must have been thousands of large, unprepossessing oil tanks fitted when oil firing was one of the cheapest methods of central heating. Now that oil is no longer so attractive, such a tank could be replaced with a galvanised water tank, carefully screened or covered with climbing plants, in order to catch the water from all roofs, including sheds, summerhouses, greenhouses, and fuel stores. It would even be possible to use the original oil tank if it were steam cleaned and painted to protect from corrosion. I am sure that there will come a time, as the cost of water becomes a more important factor, when such bulk water storage will become an accepted policy for the houseowner.

Such bulk water storage tanks as I have described above would be permanently connected to the gutters of the house. However, there are devices on the market that can be inserted in the downpipe in order to divert water into a rainwater butt or even larger storage systems.

In times of drought it is not unusual to find gardeners using bath water on their plants because, once cool, it is perfect for use in the garden. It is possible to store such domestic water when rainwater is no longer available and, if the storage system is fitted with a root watering system as I have described above, watering of plants is simplicity itself. By fitting a diverting valve on the bath outlet so that it can supply the garden water storage system, it is possible to supply cooled bath water direct to the roots of plants at all times of the year. Ordinary household soaps will not harm plants and if you are concerned, a simple, replaceable or washable filter could be fitted. The only water that should not be used is that from the dishwasher and washing machine, as some detergents contain chemicals that are harmful to plants. This would also apply if a chemical was used to clean the bath.

CHAPTER THREE

Garden Design

Our England is a garden that is full of stately views,
Of borders, beds and shrubberies and lawns and avenues,
With statues on the terraces and peacocks strutting by,
But the glory of the garden lies in more than meets the eye.
Rudyard Kipling, *The Glory of the Garden*

In this modern, man-made world, we are constantly surrounded by good
and bad design; it is an integral part of our lives. Although we are all
aware when we think a design is good or bad, how often do we take the
time to ask, what *is* good or bad design? In this chapter I shall try to
establish some of the elements and principles of general design and suggest
how they can be used to improve the gardens surrounding the places in
which we live and work.

Good design, whether it be of gardens, furniture, clothing or the hundreds of other items with which we surround ourselves, must satisfy a
number of important criteria.

Designing for a Purpose

One of the most important factors for the designer to keep in mind is that
any design must serve the purpose for which it is to be used. It is useless,
for instance, having a beautiful, high-performance sports car that can
travel at 150 miles an hour if you only want it to pop up to your local
shops. If one applies the same principle to the design of a garden, it is

imperative that consideration be given to the demands that the life style of the owner and family will place upon it.

The special considerations which must be given to each garden should include the funds available for design, construction and planting; the individual requirements of all family members, including children and pets; the amount of disruption and inconvenience permissible during construction; the time available for maintenance, and any particular likes and dislikes. In addition, the overall style of the garden is an important consideration. This is not always a case of simple preference, as the style may be greatly influenced by the garden's location and shape; the demands that will be placed upon it and the amount of time available to maintain it. For instance, the well-designed, formal garden may be perfect, in theory, for the person who has a very neat and tidy nature. However, formal gardens require a great deal of maintenance and are not suitable for a young, energetic family.

As the construction of a garden is far from cheap, and is also often very expensive to alter once complete, it is important that the requirements are fully established, by all members of the family, before any design is undertaken. It is best to commence by listing all the items required. Figure 2 shows a list which has been completed for a family of four with one dog. Such a list should be used as a guide only; standard items should be altered and adapted as required, and other items added if necessary.

Although it is possible to adapt a garden design to a growing family, it is important to look ahead to future family needs. For example, a family with very young children may be wise to allow a fairly large area of lawn for ball games when the children are older. Later, when the children leave home, the lawn can be subdivided or reduced by creating additional beds and borders. It is even possible to design seemingly fixed items so that they can be put to different uses in the future. The sand pit may become a formal or informal pool; the secret playground an area for nature and wildlife.

When moving into a house with an established garden, it is best to refrain from any redesign for at least a year. This allows you to record how the gardens looks through all four seasons and, by making notes and taking photographs throughout the year, any necessary alterations and developments will be highlighted.

CLIENT   ME & MRS PAGE   DATE   MARCH 1990

GARDEN CHECKLIST

Proposed Overall Style

Formal   (Yes)/No Adj House   Informal   (Yes)/No Main garden .

Use Of Garden

Extension to House	(Yes)/No	Entertaining	(Yes)/No
Sitting Area In Sun	(Yes)/No	In Shade	(Yes)/No
Children's Play area	(Yes)/No	Sports area	Yes/(No)

Items To Be Included

Entrance Drive	(Yes)/No	Vegetable Garden	(Yes)/No Raised Beds
Garage	Yes/(No)	Washing Line	(Yes)/No
Greenhouse	(Yes)/No	Water Feature	(Yes)/No
Shed	(Yes)/No	Swimming Pool	Yes/(No)
Area for Dog	(Yes)/No	Area For Bonfire	Yes/(No)
Fruit Cage	(Yes)/No	Coal/Wood Store	Yes/(No)
Patio	(Yes)/No	Children's Playhouse	(Yes)/No
Built In Barbeque	(Yes)/No	Sandpit or Swings	Yes/(No)
Summer House	Yes/(No)	Tennis Court	Yes/(No)
Croquet Lawn	Yes/(No)	Pergola or Trellis	(Yes)/No
Garden Lighting	(Yes)/No	Conservatory	(Yes)/No
Compost Area	(Yes)/No	Arbour For Climbers	(Yes)/No
Area For Dustbin	(Yes)/No		

Family Details

Number Of Adults	Male 1	Female 1	
Number Of Children	Boys 0	Girls 2	
Ages of Children			7 & 5

Fig. 2. Example of a completed garden checklist

FOCAL POINTS

The importance of a strong focal point in a painting or drawing was first impressed on me at the age of twelve by an old, and much disliked, art master. As his words, 'It-needs-a-stronger-point-of-focus-boy' were punctuated with the edge of a ruler on the top of my head, the lesson has remained with me ever since.

Although I do not use such drastic methods in my teaching (some of my students are much bigger than I am), I always try to impress on my garden design students the importance of a strong focal point in the design of a garden or landscape. A carefully and well-chosen focal point will establish scale, determine the sight line the designer prefers and draw the viewer into the garden. A garden without a focal point will have very little form and will appear to be simply a collection of plants and structures.

Items used to form the focal point will depend on the size and style of the garden, but could include statues, jardinières, urns, planters, sundials, a flight of rising steps (if they were going down, you would not be able to see them), garden furniture, structures such as summerhouses, arbours, gazebos and follies, a water feature, and specimen trees and shrubs.

Where a part of the garden is out of sight it is often possible to place a focal point with a definite shape, such as a seat, so that only a part of it may be seen. This will make the viewer aware that there is literally more to the garden than at first meets the eye, and increase the wish to investigate – an important element if the garden is to be interesting. This does not work with trees and shrubs, however, because they simply blend into the background.

In cases where the above, partly seen focal point is inappropriate, it is important that the focal point remains unobstructed, or it may complicate the picture. It is possible to 'borrow' a pleasant focal point from outside the garden. Examples are a neighbour's summerhouse or gazebo, a church tower, or an attractive specimen tree. Such a 'picture' will often be improved by planting trees and shrubs so as to frame the view. Care must be taken, when using focal points outside the garden, not to have items within the garden that will compete and complicate the picture. For instance, if there is a view of a church tower outside the garden, but an eye-catching seat within, the latter may be intrusive and spoil the effect.

In a fairly large garden, where it is possible to 'perambulate' from one area to another, the selection and location of focal points becomes of the

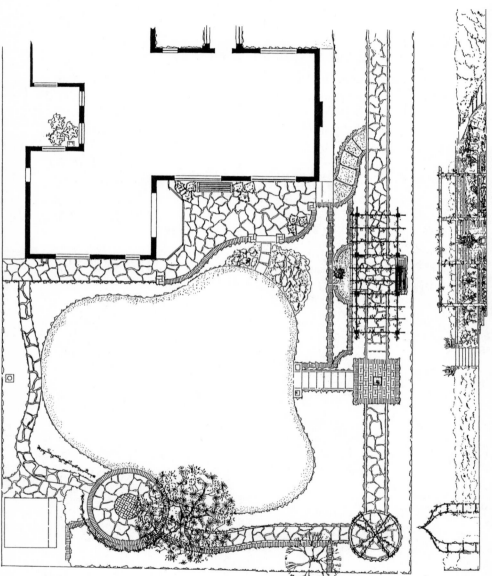

Fig. 3. A garden design indicating a sequence of focal points

utmost importance. As an example, in the garden design illustrated in figure 3 the initial focal point from the terrace next to the house is the large, circular, paved area beneath the tree. Having moved to this position, the interest is taken by the rose arbour to the left of the garden; from the arbour, the eye is attracted along the path to the bird bath on the square, paved area, and one then has a choice of either climbing the steps and crossing the lawn or carrying on through the pergola, with the opportunity to sit for a while in the dappled shade. Such carefully selected and placed focal points make a walk around this garden both interesting and satisfying and give the impression of increased size.

The above diagram also illustrates the need for a carefully designed base line from which to view the point of focus. In figure 3 the setting-off point from the house terrace towards the point of focus – the circular paved area – is established by the paving slabs in the scree garden: the edge of the slab which is against the edge of the lawn is carefully aligned with the circular terrace. Had the terrace been placed two metres to the left, the position of the entry of the slabs from the scree bed would have had to be altered to suit. This linking of focal point and base line is very important and should be carefully established within even the smallest design.

The focal point should harmonise with the overall style of the garden and should also fit the proportions of the design. For example, a very large, Italianate statue in a traditional English or cottage garden will seem very much out of place. Likewise, a small concrete statue will be out of proportion if set amongst mature trees and shrubs.

The material chosen for a focal point is also very important. Modern materials, such as plastic and fibreglass, sit unhappily in the informal atmosphere of a country garden but are perfect for a more formal courtyard garden; the white-painted seat used as a focal point in a woodland walk will always be out of place. Far better in such a position to use an old tree trunk which has been carved to the rough shape of a seat. There is a vast selection of materials available. For the more informal situation, wood, stone and concrete may be appropriate, whilst in a formal garden, ter-racotta, plastic, fibreglass, bronze and ceramics could be used. It is, however, the style and shape of the item, rather than the material, which will establish its suitability as a focal point.

SCALE

When teaching the principle of scale to garden design students I often use the example of the teapot (see figure 4). As can be seen, the teapot possesses all its relevant parts, namely the bowl, base, handle, spout and lid, and there is a hole in the top for water. However, because the parts have not been designed to the same scale, the teapot is unusable. The base is so small that the teapot will not stand without support; the spout is so long that the tea will come over the rim of the bowl before it pours from the spout. The handle is far too small to be practical; this also applies to the knob on the lid. Good design would have required that all the parts of the teapot were considered in relation to each other and to the purpose for which it, as a whole, was designed.

Fig. 4. An out-of-scale teapot

The same principles of scale apply to the design of a landscape or garden. The garden will consist of a collection of items such as paving, walls, fences, steps, pergolas and arches, garden buildings such as a shed, green-house or summerhouse, pools and, of course, trees, shrubs and other plants. In the same way that, with the teapot, the handle must relate both to the size of the bowl and to the hand that is to hold it, all such garden items should relate to each other in scale. This will affect the choice of focal points, the relationship of the height of steps to their tread, the height and width of pergolas and arches, the selection of plants and trees and the choice and style of garden buildings and structures.

The scale of any landscape will either be to human scale or to the scale of nature as it is very difficult to combine the two without drastically affecting the overall atmosphere. For instance, if we consider the scale of an average house, we immediately see that it is built to accommodate the average human being: the rooms, stairs, doorways, windows, etc. are all to human scale. If well designed, this gives an atmosphere of comfort and homeliness. However, in the stately home or the premises of a large institution, we find a scale that is far larger than human. There are high walls, wide windows and doorways, and the broad sweep of the stairs that are designed to impress. Although such buildings may be beautiful and awe-inspiring, they do not offer the same atmosphere of comfort and homeliness as does the house built to human scale. This same principle may be applied to the design of the garden. In a garden where one wishes to relax in comfort, it is important that all items included are to human scale.

THE EFFECT OF VOLUME AND SPACE IN GARDEN DESIGN

It is a common fault for those who are new to garden design to begin by establishing the shape and size of the various masses in the garden, such as beds, borders or summerhouses. In this way they are attempting to establish the volume of the beds and borders before considering the space that will be created between them. For it is the spaces between masses that will greatly affect the overall character and atmosphere of the garden, and the way we react to it. For instance, a wide path with space either side has the effect of lulling one into a feeling of comfort and security and will induce a leisurely stroll. By comparison, a narrow path between large shrubs or trees causes one to move quickly to a more open area.

Shapes, too, within planted areas cause different atmospheres and reactions. The circle is a very comfortable shape, especially if seating is provided around the edges and there is some focal point, such as a statue or sundial, in the centre. This arrangement is very static and will induce a wish to remain within the area. Squares and even more complicated shapes, such as hexagons and octagons, cause restlessness and the wish to move on. For example, a triangular-shaped area with a path leading towards one of the corners will have the effect of increasing the speed of someone walking along the path. Landscape designers will often use the knowledge of the effect of such shapes in their designs, especially in public spaces where they wish to influence the movement of pedestrians. Such knowledge is also useful when planning the character and atmosphere of each area within a garden.

In figure 5 a fairly large garden has been divided to create separate 'rooms'. Because of the various shapes, each room has a different atmosphere and purpose; taken as a whole, they make the garden seem much larger than it really is. Anyone who has visited a house at the oversight stage of construction will know how small the floor plan appears. Once the walls are built, however, the individual rooms appear much larger, thus giving the impression of increased overall size. Subdividing the garden has a similar effect.

It is important, when creating garden 'rooms', that the materials chosen to mark each area's perimeter are the correct height. In order to establish an individual area, the surrounding barrier, whether it be a fence, wall or evergreen planting, must extend to at least eye-height. Anything below this level will look like nothing but tall ground cover.

When approaching the design of the garden, one must first establish the atmosphere that is required for each area. The space between masses within the area may then be created to provide the required ambience. If a very formal tone is wanted, strict geometric shapes created by fencing or paving will provide a suitable framework for planting. It is often advisable, and effective, to soften such formality with planting of a more informal nature, such as the massed planting of evergreen and deciduous shrubs together with some herbaceous plants. As formal gardens are generally smaller than informal gardens, I find that shrubs with large leaves such as *Fatsia japonica* and *Hosta sieboldiana* 'Elegans' are very successful at softening strict formality when combined with plants such as ferns and ivies.

Within informal gardens, the spaces between the masses may be created by areas of lawn or low ground cover. By placing such areas of low ground cover around a lawn, it is possible to give an impression of greater space, which stretches into the adjacent borders. Since informal gardens should comprise flowing lines and curves, it is best to soften the straight lines of any fences or walls with plants that grow above eye level. Such plants may be thought of as 'structural', as they will establish the shape of the garden.

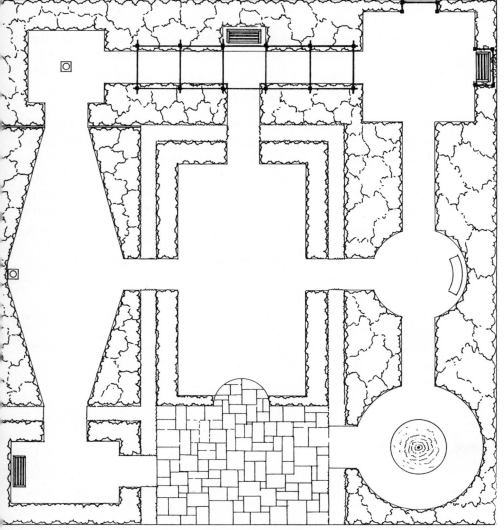

Fig. 5. Garden 'rooms' of various shapes

Another important element which will affect the space within a garden is what can be seen of something outside it. Where a garden overlooks an impressive view, it will be beneficial to the design to incorporate the view, as has been mentioned above. However, where there is an unsightly view, it may be necessary to plant tall shrubs or trees to hide it. This will have an immediate effect on the space within the garden and the design must be adapted accordingly.

ESTABLISHING THE STYLE

The example of the teapot, used previously to illustrate the need for scale in a design, is also useful in showing the importance of establishing the correct style. In figure 6 the teapot is made up of various styles, both formal and informal. The bowl is informal, glazed earthenware, whilst the spout and handle are very formal, one in silver, the other in copper. The knob on the lid is extremely ornate, whilst the base is made of plain, stained wood. Whilst this hybrid teapot is made up of good, well-designed parts, each wholly acceptable in their own right, the mixture of styles gives a totally undesirable result.

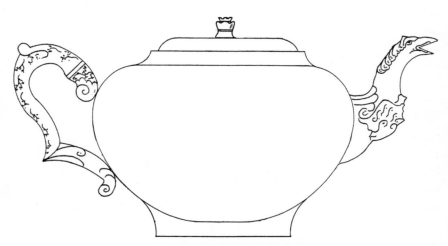

Fig. 6. Teapot showing various styles

Although often not quite so obvious, mixtures of styles in the garden can be ultimately as inappropriate: for instance, siting a very ornate stone statue close to a half-barrel filled with annuals, or a square, formal flowerbed edged with clipped box in the centre of an informal lawn.

Landscape and garden designers usually think of style as either formal or informal. Formal design is epitomised by squares, rectangles and circles, whereas informal design is achieved by more flowing, irregular lines and informal planting. Within the garden it is usual to find both styles, especially if the garden is fairly large, but care must be taken when progressing from one style to another. Lancelot 'Capability' Brown, the ultimate lover of informality, did away with all the elements of formality from the previous age and brought the countryside right up to the house. However, Humphrey Repton, who followed him, improved the design around the house by reintroducing the terrace in order to add an element of formality. This was necessary because the house itself is formal. The plan of most houses is rectangular, as are the doors and windows.

Today, it is usual to provide an area of paving next to the house to give a safe, dry area for sitting or as access. The formality of such paving may be softened, but not spoilt, by making use of interesting patterns of paving, or by softening the edges of the paving with planting. Moreover, the formality imposed by the house can be reduced as one progresses into the garden. The terrace may flow into a flowerbed, which in turn flows into an informal lawn that is bordered at the far end by a planting of informal trees.

UNITY IN THE DESIGN

With forms of art, such as painting, architecture and fabric design, it may be assumed that the design is at its most perfect the moment it is finished. By comparison, while it is very difficult to establish when a garden is at its best, it may be assumed that it will improve as it matures. In addition, the seasonal alterations that take place in plants and trees will result in vast changes in the atmosphere and 'feel' of the garden. It is therefore imperative that the different aspects of the garden are united in concept so as to hold the atmosphere together throughout the year.

Unity within the garden may be achieved by first establishing a concept and then ensuring that all elements conform to it. There are some 'conceptual' styles which are so well established that a single word will summon up a vision of that style: the Japanese garden, for instance, or the Italian garden, or the cottage garden. However, even if one is not working to such strict rules, it is important to establish a basic concept within the design and ensure all items of both hard and soft landscaping are selected to suit. Thus the choice of complementary materials for paving, walling or steps, and the selection and location of trees and plants to enhance the overall 'theme' will ensure the garden is a unity.

Hard Landscaping

This term generally refers to anything in the garden which is not growing, and includes paving, walling, fencing, ornaments and steps. Hard landscaping is difficult to change and matures relatively slowly, so it must be used with great care. It also eats up a high proportion of the cost of most gardens, and any mistakes at the design stage can be costly to rectify once construction is complete.

If the garden is to be pleasant and harmonious, it is also important that a particular theme is maintained throughout. Thus a type of paving, such as basket weave, brickwork or random, reconstituted York stone, once chosen for the drive or terrace, should be included in other areas of the garden. However, it is possible to change the ratio of two materials and still maintain the harmony of design. For instance, the drive may be constructed of York stone paving with brick edging; the terrace of panels of York stone surrounded with brick; and a path to the summerhouse paved in alternate panels of brick and York stone. This principle applies equally to fencing, walls and other structures.

There are many interesting materials that can be used in the garden and, fortunately, the dull concrete paths which once surrounded thousands of houses in this country are now being replaced by more exciting and pleasant textures. As long as the concept of harmony is kept in mind, it is possible to incorporate anything from real or reconstituted stone to flint, slate, wood and metalwork.

The style of walling and paving may also be greatly influenced by the bonding pattern chosen. For instance, square stone paving, basket-weave brickwork, herring-bone brickwork, and interlinked hexagonal paving are all formal, whilst broken stone paving, random stone paving and gravel are more informal. Similarly, with walling, traditional brickwork in stretcher, English or Flemish bond will appear fairly formal, whilst a dry-stone wall or a flint wall will look informal. It must also be remembered that some bonding patterns are more directional than others: for example, basket-weave brickwork is static; herring-bone brickwork is directional. As such directional paving will affect the 'line' of the design, it must be given much thought before both the material and pattern are chosen.

Fencing, too, will affect both the style of the garden and the environment adjacent to the fence, and should be selected with care. Fences erected as windbreaks should not present a solid barrier to the prevailing wind, as vertical, close-boarded or interwoven panels do, but should 'filter' the air. Thus a close-trellis or hit-and-miss fencing will create a much better environment downwind of the fence. As far as style is concerned, formal trelliswork and metal fencing may be painted to add to the formality, but the colours should be chosen to harmonise with the overall design and the colours of adjacent planting. More informal trellis may be used to grow climbers which, if allowed to develop fully, may ultimately completely obscure their support. Since formal trellis is chosen more for its architectural effect, it is not usual to obscure it fully with planting, although the strict lines may be softened by planting less vigorous climbing roses or other easily controlled plants.

Other hard landscaping items, such as pergolas, arbours, pools, and lighting, will add interest to the garden but, again, they must be chosen so as to suit the overall design. Thus the support of a pergola may be constructed of the same brick as the adjacent paving and the stones used to edge the pool may be made of the same material as the adjacent rock garden. As some of the structures in the garden are quite large, other important factors, mentioned elsewhere in this chapter, must not be forgotten. These include the need to maintain scale and proportion and to ensure balance in the design.

THE CHILDREN'S GARDEN

I have recommended that all members of the family be kept in mind when designing the garden, which may mean including an area where children can play without causing damage to plants or garden structures, or annoying the neighbours. It is also a good idea to provide a small area where children can have their own garden. One only has to see the excitement on the face of a child who has grown some watercress in a pot on the kitchen windowsill to see how enjoyable growing things can be to children. I well remember a visit to a client which was dominated by a lecture from a six-year-old on how she had grown such a tall sunflower.

We all know how much more satisfying it is to sit down to a home-grown meal, but for a child the magic lies in discovering how flowers and vegetables grow from a tiny seed to a plant larger than themselves. Such experiences at a young, influential age can often have far-reaching effects and there are many professional gardeners, garden designers and landscape architects who owe their careers to their first small garden.

If you allocate an area of ground to a child there are a number of things to keep in mind.

First, don't be tempted to give over the dry, poor area in deep shade, where nothing will grow, as this will only discourage your child and may put him off gardening for ever. Far better to select an open but protected area in sun, where the plants will develop quickly. Prepare the ground well as described in chapter one and ensure that your child, too, sees the need for good preparation.

Encourage your child to use quick-growing plants with either bright colours or large leaves that will show fast, impressive results.

Make sure that the children are safe by giving them tools that are easy to handle, and show them how to use them properly.

Show them how to water plants correctly, as described in chapter two. (This may be an excellent opportunity to teach young children the need to preserve water by setting up a simple root-watering system from an adjacent water container.)

Ensure the garden is protected from pets and wildlife. Children can become greatly attached to a garden or even a particular plant and can be very disappointed if it is damaged by a cat, next door's dog or a visiting badger.

If you have more than one child, try to allocate an area of garden to each. Sharing a garden is hard enough for an adult, but for children it is almost impossible.

Show the child the importance of order in the garden, of cleanliness and of checking on the plants every day. Keeping an eye on a small area of garden for a short period each day can be an excellent discipline.

Last but not least, take an interest in your child's garden. Share some of your time and listen to any points the child may raise. You will find your own joy in gardening is refreshed through the new eyes of your son or daughter.

XERISCAPING

Any book about saving water in the garden must include something on xeriscaping, which originated in the southwest of the United States of America and is a type of landscape design about which very little is known in Britain at present. It developed out of the need to save water and makes use of items of hard landscaping such as rocks, cobbles, gravel, slate and wood to form an almost maintenance-free design. In the United States it is unusual to find manufactured materials, such as brick, in the design as the aim is to make the landscape appear as natural as possible. Only drought-resistant plants are incorporated and are used sparingly as points of focus.

Whilst this type of design may be considered uninteresting when compared with some traditional forms of planting, it does have its benefits and can be quite attractive if well constructed. For instance, the design may be such as to give an impression of movement. Thus, small rocks or cobbles may be placed so as to represent a flowing river or a lake out of which larger rocks may protrude. Slates placed on edge may represent water falling over a rock and gravel may be integrated with stone to provide interesting variations in texture.

If this type of design grows in popularity in this country, we may find that other materials, such as brick, ceramics and metal, are incorporated. Such materials are popular for paving in our gardens and could easily be integrated into the relatively smaller areas around our homes.

CHAPTER FOUR

Designing with Plants

I have seen one clambering rose, one lingering hollyhock glorify a cottage home, arrest one's step, and prolong one's meditation, more than all the terraces of Chatsworth.
Alfred Austin

As far as a garden designer is concerned, a plant or group of plants can be treated in exactly the same way as all the other items in the garden. Like a wall, a flight of stone steps, an arch or a pergola, plants and trees provide a mass which has shape, form, texture, colour and light-reflective or absorption properties. The aim of the garden designer is to integrate suitable plants into the design so as to complement and unite the elements of hard landscaping.

THE PRINCIPLES OF PLANTING DESIGN

The basic principles employed when designing with plants are the same as those for other forms of art such as architecture, interior design, fabric design, or sculpture. Before one can create any aesthetic composition, one should be conscious of these principles and how they may be employed.

The Use of Line Within a Garden

When designing even the smallest garden, one must first establish the lines which will be created and the form that will result. The lines within a garden are created by the planting of evergreen trees and shrubs and the location of paths, fences and pergolas. In rural locations, where the garden is open to the countryside, the lie of the adjacent land may greatly influence the line of the garden which, in turn, will affect the complete design.

As straight lines are emphatically directional, they will lead the eye to the meeting point of another, intersecting line. In such a situation the focal point is placed at the intersection of the two lines formed by the avenue of trees. Thus the natural line of the garden is enhanced and strengthened by the inclusion of a strong focal point. In some situations, however, it may be necessary to break up a dominant line that is spoiling the shape of the garden. Figure 7 illustrates how a garden with a sloping horizon may be improved by planting tall trees and introducing a strong focal point.

Shape and Form

Within the landscape, form is established by the shape of the land and by the masses created by the planting of groups of trees and shrubs. Whilst a single tree may be narrow and vertical, a large group of the same trees may produce an almost straight, horizontal line against the sky, in which case the 'form' of the planting would be a rectangle. As form will greatly influence the atmosphere of a garden, it should be carefully considered at an early stage of the design. Mature plants have various forms, including fastigiate (*Taxus baccata* 'Fastigiata Aurea'), round (*Thuja occidentalis* 'Woodardii'), pyramidal or conical (*Picea glauca* 'Albertiana Conica'), square or rectangular ('Pleached trees), spiky (foliage of *Yucca gloriosa*), domed or fan-shaped (*Prunus mume*). When extremely geometric, such strict forms may be considered 'architectural', as they will appear more dominant within the planting than other, more irregular-shaped plants. Such architectural plants may be used to give emphasis to a particular location and provide a point of focus. This effect may be highlighted by

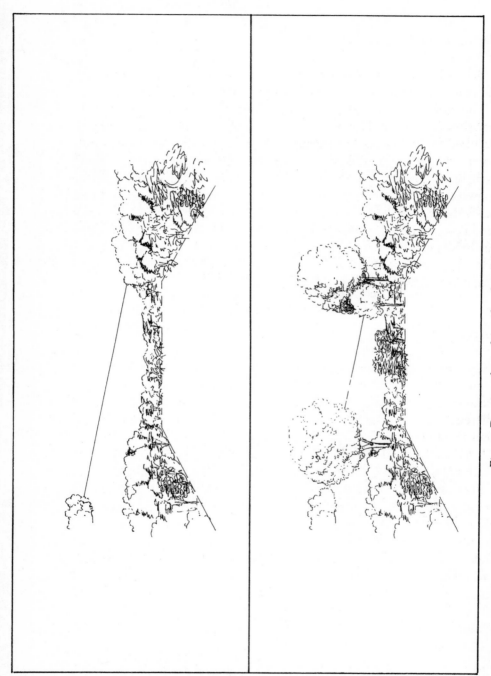

Fig. 7. *Drawing of a garden with a sloping horizon*

placing the plant against a brick wall or other planting of a different colour or texture.

Before leaving the subject of shape and form one must consider how the growing habit of an individual plant will affect the garden design.

The growing habit of any plant is dependent on the arrangement of its branches and stems. However, when in leaf, the plant's habit may be disguised by its foliage. For example, the shape of the deciduous shrub, *Cornus alba*, when in full leaf is an irregular hummock, whilst the habit of its stems is vertical. Care must be taken, therefore, to ensure that the shape of the deciduous shrub chosen for its summer foliage will also satisfy the overall design during the winter. The habit may be weeping or pendulous, arching, vertical, horizontal or spreading, or irregular, but the true habit of a plant or tree is often not obvious until it comes to maturity, so it is important to check with a plant catalogue or with the nursery prior to making a purchase.

Texture

There is an excellent opportunity, within the design of a garden, to include elements of both hard and soft landscaping which will provide interesting textural variety. Plants and trees can be selected which have leaves of different size, shape and form; in addition, the light absorption or reflective qualities of plants will greatly affect texture and colour.

In general, interesting effects can be created by incorporating plants which have foliage of contrasting textures. Thus, the scintillating texture of *Euonymus fortunei* set against the leathery leaves of *Viburnum davidii* provides interest both in colour and texture. In hard landscaping, the shape, size and pattern of various areas of brick, stone, gravel or wood will provide contrasting textures. Thus, a popular style of paving is an area of random, rectangular, York stone paving with a brick edge, which provides both textural and colour contrast. Another example, for a more informal setting, is the use of fine gravel with a timber surround constructed of old railway sleepers. Care should be taken when choosing the pattern and texture of paving as they will greatly influence movement. For instance, square paving and, to a lesser extent, broken-stone (crazy) paving, are static, whilst hexagonal paving and rectangular stone slabs placed length-ways have a lengthening effect. The same slabs placed crossways, however, will have a broadening effect and reduce the impression of movement.

Balance

Although true balance is almost impossible to achieve within the garden, except for extremely formal gardens that are perfectly symmetrical, it is important to bear it in mind. A landscape or garden which has a large mass to one side will be imbalanced and any further design work should include ways to correct the fault. For instance, a garden with a massed planting of trees to the left will require some other mass to the right. This does not necessarily have to be further planting, but could be a pergola or series of rose arches.

The concept of balance may also be used when considering the relationship of hard to soft landscaping. One of my much respected garden design colleagues has a saying that, 'The grey should never outweigh the green', meaning that soft landscaping, such as lawns, plants and trees, should never be dominated by hard landscaping like paving, walling or pergolas. By following this dictum we can ensure that the garden is soft and welcoming at all times of the year. This concept of balance between the major elements of the garden is at the heart of good garden design.

Integration and Grouping of Plants

Thanks to the influence of garden designers from a previous age, such as William Robinson and Gertrude Jekyll, it is now accepted practice to plant species in drifts which relate to adjacent plants in both colour and texture. Such planting gives an atmosphere of order to beds and borders and creates a sense of establishment, even to a newly planted garden. However, whilst the massed planting of dozens of the same species of shrub may be satisfactory for the planting around office buildings and hospitals, care should be taken to avoid monotony within the smaller area of a garden. One must beware of too much repetition in a planting scheme and ensure there is sufficient variety to maintain interest.

COLOUR

Today, colour is recognised as one of the most important aspects in all forms of design. However, unlike the selection of colour for interior design, fabrics or fashion, the colours and associated atmosphere within a garden will change constantly.

Whilst our response to colour depends greatly on our emotional make-up, it is generally accepted that the warm and hot colours – red, orange and yellow – inflame the emotions, whilst the cool colours – green, blue and mauve – are more restful. Within the landscape and garden, however, there is an additional aspect to be considered. Since the intensity of light throughout the day and seasons greatly influences how colours appear to us, thought must be given to the required colour effect for a given location. The more intense the light, the stronger the actual colour needs to be to be seen to best effect. For instance, pastel shades look feeble at noon but towards dusk they show up more and more. In much stronger light, pastel shades appear to have almost no colour at all. When designing with plants, one must consider how much light a plant, or group of plants, will receive, and select accordingly.

It must also be remembered that colour in the landscape is not seen in isolation but in relation to all the colours around it. These include the vast ranges of greens, the various blues and greys of the sky and the myriad colours associated with the other plants. Colours in the landscape and garden are constantly changing. In addition to the effect of light as it changes during the day and the seasons, there is also the constant change of plants as they grow and develop. Even items of hard landscaping such as paving, walls and fences change their colour and character as they mature.

How colours relate to each other is best illustrated in the colour or spectral wheel. Figure 8 shows the wheel in one of its most basic forms. This comprises the three primary colours: red, yellow, and blue, with three secondary colours: green, orange and purple, and six intermediate colours formed by mixing yellow with orange, yellow with green, blue with green, blue with purple, red with purple and red with orange. Additional colours can be obtained by mixing two adjacent colours and some spectral wheels consist of hundreds of different hues. However, no matter how complicated it may be, the exciting thing about the spectral wheel is that it shows the relationships between colours by their position around the wheel.

First, there is the harmony of adjacent colours. If one has blue as a dominant colour, for instance, then blue mixed with green and blue mixed with purple will harmonise. Second, there is the contrast of opposite colours: yellow with purple, orange with blue, red with green. . . . Thirdly, there is the harmony of triads. For example, if we take yellow as the initial colour, then the triad harmony colours are red and blue.

As with every guideline, principle or rule, the spectral wheel should be followed with care. For instance, the three primary colours, if used in their most dominant forms, will overpower any other colour included with them, even if those colours are related in some way on the wheel. For that reason, modern planting practice favours the more subtle pastel shades.

PROCEDURES FOR THE SELECTION OF TREES AND PLANTS

From the above, it will be seen that trees and plants for our gardens should be selected not on a whim but to fit in with a specific design. However, the design may consist of many different aspects, all of which have to be satisfied.

The first step is to decide which trees and large shrubs will form the line and shape of the garden or landscape. This 'structural' element requires trees and shrubs which are more than 2 metres high so that they will not only provide the line of the garden and form the required shape within the hard lines of the boundary, but also act as a screen to hide poor views and provide privacy and shelter.

Having established the types of 'structural' plants that could be used, one must then consider specific aspects of each. Depending on the type of plant, this should include the ultimate height and width, the plant habit and shape, the soil conditions available, the aspect, the hardiness, the colour and any seasonal impact of foliage and flowers, the texture and light-reflective or absorption properties of the foliage, any special resistance to disease and the rate of growth. In addition, each plant must be selected so that it will complement those adjacent to it in colour, texture, form and shape, as suggested previously in this chapter.

Figure 9 gives a step-by-step guide to selecting appropriate plants for particular applications. As can be seen, a different answer to any one of the selection criteria will result in the choice of a different plant, so care should be taken at each stage.

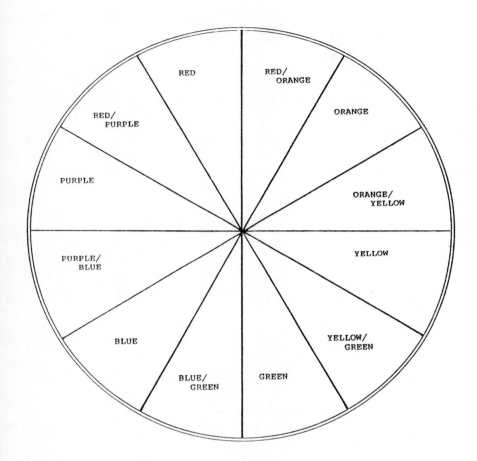

Fig. 8. The Colour Wheel

Colours adjacent to each other on the wheel are in harmony, i.e. Blue and Blue/Purple or Red and Red/Purple

Colours opposite each other on the wheel are in contrast, i.e. Blue with Orange or Red with Green

Colours at an angle across the wheel are in contrast, i.e. Purple with Green and Orange

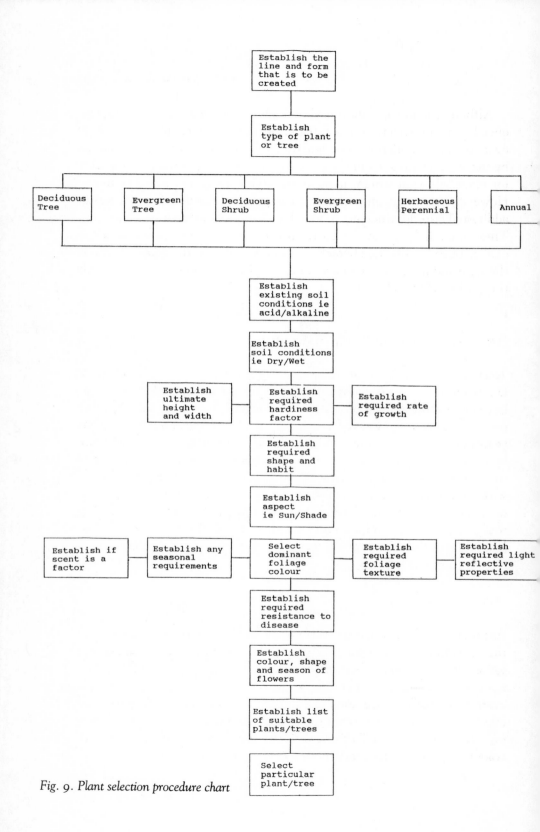

Fig. 9. Plant selection procedure chart

Although landscape architects and garden designers who are experienced in plant selection and integration may not refer to such a chart every time they undertake a design, they still subconsciously choose plants by the same process of elimination. This has led to the use of computers for plant selection which, in some instances, gives a satisfactory result. However, for a planting scheme to be truly successful, it must satisfy additional criteria which are more difficult to programme into a machine. These include how the garden relates to the adjacent countryside, the quality of the light, the character and preferences of the garden owners, the style and influence of adjacent buildings and the location from which the garden will be viewed.

AN APPROACH TO LOW-MAINTENANCE PLANTING

Today it is recognised that in the average garden, maintenance must be kept to a minimum because labour costs are now very high and people have many more and various activities to occupy their time. It is therefore necessary to discover ways of creating the garden shape and providing all-year-round planting interest whilst keeping maintenance time down. The best way, which has developed over the years, involves the integration of trees, shrubs and ground cover with hardy perennials and bulbs to provide seasonal colour. In this type of planting, the shrubs provide the background or shape, the bulbs and hardy perennials provide definite colour during the spring, summer and autumn, and the ground cover retains moisture and prevents the growth of weeds.

Structural Planting

As previously described, trees and large shrubs over two metres tall provide the structural planting for the garden. In addition to establishing the garden's overall shape, however, such planting will also provide a backdrop against which other plants can be grown. It is therefore usual to use evergreen shrubs for structural planting, as they provide an all-year-round effect. Furthermore, it is often found that deep green is an excellent foil for other plants, especially those with red flowers or stems (an example of colours opposite each other on the spectrum wheel).

There are also many beautiful evergreen and deciduous shrubs with variegated foliage, which add interest and may be used to brighten a dull border. The most common variegations are green and yellow or green and white, but there are some other interesting combinations, such as green and red, and red and purple. However, variegated foliage does place restrictions on the positioning of the plant in relation to others. For example, one should avoid placing a yellow and green plant next to a white and green one, as the white variegation will simply look washed out.

Since the trees and large shrubs chosen as structural plants will form the shape of the garden for many years to come, thought must be given to their growing requirements, as indicated earlier in this chapter. These will include whether the plant is acid or alkaline loving, whether it flourishes in sun or shade, whether it grows best in moist or well-drained soil, and whether it prefers rich or poor soil conditions. Also, some plants require protection from severe winds or frost. As structural plants will often be planted close to the boundary, it may be necessary to plant other, very hardy shrubs or trees to protect the more ornamental plants that are not sheltered by the perimeter planting, particularly if one lives in an exposed location.

When designing with shrubs, some of which are potentially very large, it is also very important that one makes sure the plant will not be out of proportion with the overall planting arrangement when fully grown. For structural planting, it is preferable to plant shrubs with a dense, closed habit, as this will create a better barrier against which other plants may grow.

The shape, size, colour and reflective qualities of the foliage should also be considered at this stage. Interest may be heightened by integrating large-leaved plants with those with fine leaves. Shrubs with round or ovate leaves act as a fine foil for those with long, narrow leaves. Some shrubs have leaves which are dull and have poor reflective properties. These act as good foils for shrubs with shiny leaves. As mentioned previously, a sombre section of planting may be brightened by incorporating shrubs with bright yellow leaves, which reflect every bit of light that falls their way. Again, though, one must ensure that the plant will grow happily in the proposed location, as some plants will not grow well in shade whilst others prefer it.

Intermediate Planting

Having established the overall shape of the garden with structural planting, one can then add some smaller evergreen and deciduous shrubs to
provide extra shape within the bed or border. As such plants will be
protected by the larger shrubs, and it is possible to make use of those which
are more ornamental both in foliage and flower, as long as the colours are
chosen carefully so that they relate to the other plants in the border. It is
also often possible to make the planting more exciting by including
shrubs with a spiky, upright habit, such as *Yucca gloriosa*. Such shrubs are
considered 'architectural' plants and may be used in a border to highlight
a particular area or to provide extra, overall interest. As with structural
planting, thought must be given to the shape, size, colour and reflective
qualities of the foliage for intermediate planting.

Having used shrubs of various sizes to give the bed or border its basic
shape, one can then integrate other plants to provide additional colour
and interest. These will include herbaceous plants, bulbs and corms, and
ground cover.

Ground Cover Planting

Whilst herbaceous planting will dominate the border throughout the late
spring, summer and autumn, there are fairly long periods during the winter
when it disappears altogether, leaving large, empty spaces. This is where
the wise selection and placing of ground cover planting comes into its
own.

Ground cover helps to deter weeds and cut down loss of moisture from
the soil. It can provide all-year-round colour and act as a superb foil to
other, larger plants. However, as ground cover plants may be in constant
shade from other, larger plants, one must make sure they have the growing
conditions they need. One must also take care that the chosen plants
reach the correct height when fully grown and will not suffocate the plants
under which they are located.

Herbaceous Planting

Herbaceous planting offers us a wide range of colour, form, shape and texture, with plants from as little as 2.5cm high to monsters of over 2m or more. Herbaceous planting is, however, very labour intensive as it requires weeding, staking or supporting, dead-heading as the flowers die, and cutting down in the winter. Despite these disadvantages, there are many herbaceous plants that thrive in very dry conditions and they can be very rewarding if one has the time to carry out the important maintenance tasks.

The main advantage with herbaceous planting is the relatively fast growth of the plants. A bed or border will develop very quickly and within two or three years will provide a dense, integrated mass of foliage and flowers. This has the double effect of reducing water loss from the soil due to evaporation and keeping down weeds. It is possible to change the location of most herbaceous plants, either in the autumn or spring, therefore any mistakes in planting or colour relationships can be easily rectified.

Bulbs and Corms

When integrating bulbs and corms into the mixed border, it is helpful to choose those that do not require raising each year and that will happily grow and multiply. Again, there is a wide variety of drought-resistant bulbs to choose from, some of which are described in the glossary at the end.

Most bulbs and corms do poorly in waterlogged soil, so good drainage is required. A little sand added to the bottom of the planting hole will mean the bulb is in contact with the soil yet has the required drainage. If bulbs and corms are to remain in position for many years, it is important that they are planted at the correct depth. It is a common fault to plant bulbs too shallow, which will result in poor growth, harm from frost and damage resulting from working the soil.

Because of the importance of maintaining colour relationships within the planting, one should establish how the colour of the plant will relate to its neighbours'. It must be remembered that many bulbs and corms produce plants that have multicoloured flowers, which can be more difficult to integrate. Where the bulb or corm produces flowers of a dominant or single colour, the relationship is easier to plan. The mass planting of bulbs is always very effective and it is possible to underplant to provide extra interest. A very good example of the combination of bulbs with other plants is red tulips with blue forget-me-nots, which often forms the basis of ornamental, municipal planting in parks and gardens. As with herbaceous planting, it is a simple matter to change the location of the bulbs or corms once you have seen how they actually relate in your own plan.

PLANTING DISTANCES OF TREES, SHRUBS AND HERBACEOUS PERENNIALS

The planting distance between trees, shrubs and herbaceous perennials has always been a contentious subject amongst garden designers and almost every designer has his or her own particular theory. Obviously, where trees and plants such as *Phormium tenax*, *Cornus contraversa* and *Chamaecyparis lawsoniana* 'Columnaris' are selected for their architectural effect, they are best seen standing proud against a complementary background. However, if the intention is to select trees and plants so that they combine to form a mass of varying colour, shape and texture, then correct planting distances become extremely important.

In theory it is possible to integrate trees and shrubs so that they overlap by between a quarter and a third of their ultimate width. This results in even integration without the dominance of one shrub over another. In practice, however, because of the relatively slow growth rate of many evergreen and deciduous shrubs, such spacing has been found to be unsatisfactory in the average garden. Many garden owners today live in their home for relatively short periods and wish to see newly planted areas of beds and borders established fairly quickly. Such theoretical planting distances as indicated above, whilst giving satisfactory cover when the shrubs are fully developed, will not provide the 'instant' integration often required.

Consider, for example, the integration of three evergreen shrubs such as *Aucuba japonica variegata*, *Garrya elliptica* and *Mahonia japonica*. These offer quite good variations in habit, shape, colour and texture and will combine well. Planning for integration of between a quarter and a third of the ultimate width would give spacings of between 1.5 and 2 metres between the plant centres. However, in practice, because of the slow growth of both the *Aucuba* and the *Mahonia* it is necessary to reduce the spacing to 1 metre or less if very quick integration is required.

The chart below indicates suggested planting distances for varying effects. However, it must be remembered that close planting distances, whilst providing better cover and integration, will involve more pruning and shaping if the planting is to remain at its best. Some of the shrubs may also need to be removed in the future if the planting becomes too overcrowded.

Suggested Planting Distances of Shrubs, Herbaceous Perennials and Ground cover

Measurements indicate the distance between the centres of plants.

Plants	Long term integration	Fairly quick integration	Very quick integration
Large shrubs	1.5m	1m	80cm
Intermediate shrubs	1m	80cm	60cm
Small shrubs	80cm	60cm	40cm
Large ground cover	1.2m	1m	80cm
Small ground cover	80cm	60cm	40cm
Large herbaceous	60cm	60cm	40cm
Small herbaceous	40cm	40cm	30cm

The above chart is an approximate guide only, which I have found useful. However, I have also found that it is important to treat each plant on its own merits. There are many good plant reference books that give the ultimate height and width of trees and shrubs, together with the relative rate of growth.

ESTABLISHING A PLANT MAINTENANCE PROCEDURE

Whilst the type of planting described above will reduce the need for day-to-day maintenance, there will still be occasional tasks to be carried out if the garden is to remain at its best. The correct preparation of the soil, the choice of suitable plants and the close integration of shrubs and ground cover will all reduce to a minimum such tasks as weeding and watering. However, as no two plants, even of the same species, ever grow exactly the same, there will always be the need for pruning and shaping, especially if potentially large shrubs have been closely spaced to provide quick integration. It may be necessary to carry out such light pruning at least once, if not twice, a year.

The maintenance plan for each plant should be established within the first year of planting. However, when pruning and shaping any individual tree or shrub, do not forget that it is to integrate with those plants around it. I have seen many excellent planting schemes spoiled by incorrect and over-zealous pruning by inexperienced gardeners.

The maintenance plan should include the full name of the tree or plant, the type and extent of the pruning to be undertaken, the best season for pruning, any necessary feeding or mulching and any dead-heading of flowers required.

CHAPTER FIVE

Lawns

And he gave it for his opinion, that whoever could make two ears of corn or two blades of grass to grow upon a spot of ground where only one grew before, would deserve better of mankind, and do more essential service to his country than the whole race of politicians put together.

Jonathan Swift, *Gulliver's Travels*

The contestants on a recent television quiz show were asked to name an evergreen hardy plant that can be mass-planted and is able to withstand very close pruning. Not one of the four contestants gave the correct answer and there were even doubtful glances towards the quizmaster when he informed them that the correct answer was 'grass'.

Grass is one of the most common plants and there are very few gardens that do not have an area of lawn. Unfortunately, it is also one of the least appreciated and most illtreated of plants in the garden. Whilst shrubs and flowers may receive regular feeding and nurture, the poor old lawn is often neglected. Within the ornamental garden in particular, however, the lawn is one of the most important elements. In the same way that a fine carpet enhances a room in a house, so the lawn sets off and completes the garden. A poorly constructed or maintained lawn will spoil even the best-designed garden. It is therefore very important to ensure the lawn is constructed and maintained so that it will stay green and healthy all year round.

Unlike other plants, which grow from their tips, grass grows from its base, so constant mowing or cropping will encourage the growth of the grasses whilst discouraging other plants in the 'lawn', whose strength of growth will be reduced. In theory, therefore, it is possible to create a lawn from any area of ground in which there is a good proportion of grasses simply by regular and correct mowing. In practice, though, it is usual to ensure correct preparation of the ground to be laid to grass and to select the grasses best suited to the expected use of the area.

TYPES OF GRASSES FOR LAWNS

The grasses which produce good lawns have a natural creeping and dwarfing habit and respond well to close mowing. A glance at a lawn seed producer's catalogue will show that each type contains a mixture of grass seeds. For instance, the mixture from a well-known supplier for golf and bowling greens contains 80 per cent chewings fescue and 20 per cent browntop bents. That is, it has a high proportion of a non-rhizomatous, relatively fine grass, which will give the high quality lawn required. However, for cricket squares, tennis courts and golf tees, which must resist wear and tear, the same supplier provides a mixture of 40 per cent amenity perennial rye-grass, 25 per cent chewings fescue, 25 per cent creeping red fescue and 10 per cent smooth-stalked meadow grass. This mixture has a greater quantity of the tougher, coarser grasses which, whilst they do not produce the fine sward of the finer varieties, are better at withstanding constant use and more irregular maintenance.

Most lawn seed suppliers will state the use for which each mixture is prepared and unless one is interested in the specific subject of grasses, it is not necessary to be aware of the habit and nature of each of a variety's constituents. However, the make-up of a mixture will determine the amount of care and maintenance required and also its resistance to drought. Furthermore, where major restructuring and conditioning of the land is not feasible, the type and condition of the soil will affect the choice of grasses to be selected for a lawn. In very wet situations, the finer grasses will be at a disadvantage because they are susceptible to damp; the red fescues, bents and meadow grasses, on the other hand, perform well on less fertile and more acid soils. Therefore, the first step in making any new lawn is to decide which type one requires. These fall into three basic categories: the utility lawn, the fine lawn and the games lawn.

If one has a growing family that requires space for ball games and cycle riding, or where regular maintenance is not readily available, the utility lawn is most suitable. This can withstand considerable wear and tear and is also fairly resistant to drought. However, as it contains a large proportion of the coarser, broad-leaved grasses, the finish will never be as fine as the other types of lawn.

The fine, or ornamental, lawn is only suitable where the lawn is grown for its visual effect, as it will not stand constant use. However, it will be up to the occasional game of bowls or croquet if given time to recover. The fine lawn does not adapt very well to long spells of drought and should only be considered if water storage, as detailed in chapter two, is provided.

The games lawn is the type used for bowling greens in constant use and requires constant, skilled care. Such a lawn is not suitable for general domestic use unless the owner has a great deal of time and interest. Even given such interest, I would still doubt its suitability for domestic use, as it requires an inordinate amount of watering.

Over recent years, many turf and lawn seed suppliers have produced varieties which complement the above three basic categories and provide many more options. Therefore, before you purchase any turf or seed, it is best to discuss your requirements, and your concern with saving water, with the supplier. Such interest will only add to the growing awareness of the need to select all plants, and especially grass, to accommodate expected drought conditions.

PROVISION OF CORRECT DRAINAGE

When preparing the ground for a new lawn which will be resistant to drought, the most important factor is the provision of good drainage. Well-drained lawns encourage the development of deep root systems and the incorporation of soil air. It may be adequate to improve drainage simply by adding coarse material, such as sand or fine gravel, to the top 15cm of soil. However, in large or difficult areas which are subject to long periods of waterlogging in winter, it may be necessary to install land drainage. Although it is possible to undertake small areas of land drainage yourself, I would suggest that specialists be involved where large areas are concerned. The typical drainage system involves the installation of either earthenware or perforated plastic pipes, buried in the ground in such a position that they gather water from the soil and convey it, by gravity, to a place where it can be dispersed. Such dispersal requires an adjacent stream, water course or ditch. If none of these are available, it may be possible to discharge into a public, surface water sewer. However, the approval of the local authority is required and they are rightly very strict on this ruling.

Over large areas, it will be necessary to provide a drainage grid in either a herring-bone or fan arrangement (see figure 10) and this is where expertise and experience is most valuable if resources are not to be wasted.

Improving the drainage of an existing lawn is, of course, much more difficult than of a new lawn and any success will depend on the extent of the problem. No amount of work undertaken on the surface will improve a badly waterlogged lawn and the only real answer is to clear the area, install proper land drainage and re-lay the lawn. However, it is often found that drainage problems in existing lawns are only caused by compaction of the surface and this may be rectified satisfactorily by spiking the lawn with a hollow-tined fork and brushing in sharp sand.

Preparation for a New Lawn

The preparation of an area to be laid to lawn is similar whether you are seeding and turfing. The area should be cleared of all perennial weeds, either by hand or by applying a weedkiller such as glyphosate at least a month prior to laying the lawn. If the lawn is to stay healthy during droughts it is important that good soil preparation and conditioning is also carried out at this stage. Such conditioning is explained in chapter one and includes double digging and the addition of organic matter, rich in nutrients. All work on lawns, but especially preparation and levelling, should be carried out when the soil is dry enough not to stick to the soles of the shoes.

The area should be roughly levelled with a rake and any large stones removed. Add or remove soil to achieve the ideal level – where a lawn abutts an area of paving, the final level of the grass should be approximately 1.5cm above the paving level for ease of mowing.

It is important at this stage that the area is firmed by walking over it, taking very short steps and pressing the heels into the surface. This operation is known as 'heeling in' and although it may appear that you are auditioning for the Ministry of Funny Walks, there is no real substitute. When the whole area is firmed, rake again and check final levels.

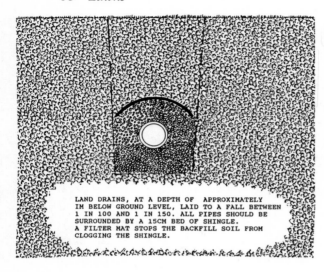

MAIN DRAIN LINES, USUALLY
15CM IN DIA, LAID APPROX
1M BELOW GROUND LEVEL TO
A FALL BETWEEN 1 IN 100 AND
1 IN 150.   MAIN DRAIN LINES
ARE APPROXIMATELY 40M APART

LATERAL CONNECTIONS, USUALLY
10CM IN DIA, LAID TO THE SAME
FALL AS THE MAIN DRAIN LINE.
LATERALS ARE POSITIONED
APPROXIMATELY 4M APART

ON LARGE DRAINAGE SYSTEMS,
INSPECTION CHAMBERS SHOULD
BE INTRODUCED APPROXIMATELY
30M APART.

LAND DRAINS, AT A DEPTH OF   APPROXIMATELY
1M BELOW GROUND LEVEL, LAID TO A FALL BETWEEN
1 IN 100 AND 1 IN 150. ALL PIPES SHOULD BE
SURROUNDED BY A 15CM BED OF SHINGLE.
A FILTER MAT STOPS THE BACKFILL SOIL FROM
CLOGGING THE SHINGLE.

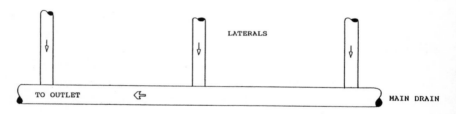

LATERALS

TO OUTLET

MAIN DRAIN

A GRID DRAINAGE SYSTEM

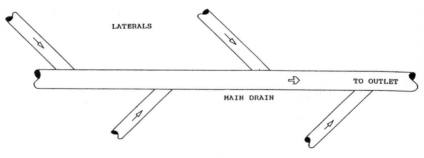

LATERALS

MAIN DRAIN

TO OUTLET

HERRINGBONE DRAINAGE SYSTEM

Fig. 10 Land drainage grids

SEED OR TURF

The advantages of laying turf are that it can be laid at most times of the year and the effect is almost instant. However, it is also very expensive compared with seeding (up to ten times the cost), is quite heavy work and must be laid within twenty-four hours of delivery. Seeding, in addition to being much cheaper, is physically much easier to do, especially on complicated lawn shapes (not that I am advocating these, because I feel they are poor design). However, it may take much longer to prepare the ground for seeding, as better surface preparation and protection against birds and cats is required.

SOWING GRASS SEED FOR LAWNS

Prior to seeding, apply a general fertiliser such as National Growmore at a rate of 50g per m² and rake into the surface. It is best to sow grass seed when it is not too wet or the surface of the lawn will be spoilt by walking on it. Choose a fairly calm day and sow as suggested by the supplier. If no sowing advice is provided, the seed may be applied at the same rate as the general fertiliser – 50g per m². It is important that the area is watered after sowing and if it is not possible to arrange a convenient shower of rain, this may be one of the few occasions when it is necessary to use a hose with a fine spray. However, if you are able to use a hose connected to a water storage system as described in chapter two, then that valuable tap water may be saved.

As grass seed is very attractive to birds, the area should be protected with netting or a makeshift scarecrow. Do not use netting with too fine a mesh or the birds will become entangled, and do not use cotton tied to sticks for the same reason. Pea sticks laid across the lawn will help to deter birds and neighbourhood cats, who seem to love rolling on newly seeded lawns.

LAYING TURF

A few days before laying turf, apply a general fertiliser such as National Growmore at a rate of 65g per m² and rake into the surface. Turf should be laid as soon as the delivery lorry leaves. If that is not possible, the turfs should be unrolled and prevented from drying out by watering and covering. However, under no situation should turfs be left longer than twenty-four hours as they will begin to deteriorate and the lawn will be affected.

Turfs are best laid from the edge of the area to be covered with at least 5cm overlap onto any adjacent paving, etc. to allow for shrinkage. Care should be taken to butt the turfs closely together and any torn edges can be trimmed with a knife. Avoid walking on newly laid turf by working from boards. The turfs can be firmed down by using the back of the rake, but do not overcompact the surface or it will spoil the aerative properties of the subsequent lawn.

If, following turf laying, there is a long period without rain, it is important to water the turf, especially along the joints. If newly laid turf begins to go brown, ensure it has good contact with the soil, carefully aerate the surface with a garden fork and apply water to the area.

It is best not to use a newly turfed lawn for anything up to six weeks, depending on how the turfs have established.

Mowing the Lawn

Any new lawn laid to turf should be left for at least four weeks before it is mowed, and even then great care must be taken not to mow closer than 2.5cm. Once any signs of the joints between the turfs have disappeared and the lawn is obviously established, the cut may be reduced to between 1.5cm and 2cm, depending on the type and finish of the grass; some of the rye-grasses, for instance, accept close mowing. It is important, however, not to mow too short in drought conditions, as this will affect the resistance of the lawn.

A newly seeded lawn must not be cut until it is at least 5cm tall, and even then the grass should only be topped. The first cut is often best done with very sharp shears if the area is not too large, but the mower may be used with care. Once the lawn is fully established, the cut may be reduced to between 1.5cm and 2cm, as above.

In summer, unless there is a drought, the lawn should be mown at least once a week and preferably twice if time allows. This will encourage proper growth and development of the lawn and increase resistance to drought.

On an established lawn it is helpful to brush the lawn with a besom broom prior to mowing as this will drag up the grass stems to meet the mower and disperse any dried worm casts.

It is important, if ridging is to be avoided, that the lawn is cut in different directions each time, that is, successive cuts are made at right angles to the previous cut.

One of the most common faults in lawn maintenance is to cut the grass too short. Although this is often done to save time, it creates major problems that can outweigh any advantages of timesaving. Close mowing results in a thin, open lawn which is an ideal environment for weeds, including clover and moss. Irregular cutting will also result in a weakened lawn with low resistance to drought and other problems.

On a cylinder mower, the height of the cut can be checked by placing a straight piece of wood across the front and rear rollers. The wood's position can then be checked against the edge of the blades. The height of the cut on a rotary mower is established in a similar way, but with the wood placed across the outside edges of the blade case. Please note: mower blades are very sharp and seem to have a will of their own, so great care should be taken at all times when using, cleaning or checking any mower. The lawn mower should be kept sharp and the balance checked at least once a year. Any work on the mower is best undertaken in the autumn, when the mower mechanic is least busy. One is then able to smile sagely when everyone else has to wait weeks, or even months, to have their mower serviced in early summer.

MAINTAINING AND IMPROVING AN ESTABLISHED LAWN

The decision whether to attempt to re-establish an existing lawn or to start again greatly depends on the condition of the existing turf. If it comprises mainly moss, daisies, clover and other weeds, the application of a weedkiller will probably result in a lawn that appears worse than before work was started. However, with regular maintenance, there are a number of ways in which a lawn with a high proportion of grasses may be improved.

Raking

Lawns which are regularly dressed and mown without a grass box are prone to a build-up of material amongst the grass shoots. This build-up is known as 'thatching', which is an excellent description as it restricts the penetration of water and air to the soil.

Thatching may be greatly discouraged by raking in the spring to remove all such material. It is best to use a multi-tined, wire, lawn rake, which is specially designed for the purpose, and sufficient pressure should be applied so as to remove the moss, old grass, etc. without pulling out the lawn grass. It is often astonishing how much unwanted material is removed, which is excellent for composting.

Aerating

Overcompaction of the soil beneath the lawn will restrict the flow of valuable rainwater to the grass roots. Such compaction may be prevented by spiking the lawn with a garden fork or a hollow-tined fork made specially for the job. The fork should be inserted into the lawn in an upright position and pressed down to a depth of at least 15cm. This should be carried out all over the lawn at intervals of 10cm. Where the hollow-tined fork is used, the cores removed from the tines may be taken to the compost heap and the holes filled by brushing in sharp sand mixed with good compost. Where there are very large areas of lawn requiring aeration, it is possible to purchase or hire aerating machines, which one simply pushes over the area.

Feeding

Lawns which are constantly cut throughout the growing season require regular feeding if they are to remain at their best. The three mineral elements required are nitrogen, phosphorus and potassium. The use of fertilisers is described in chapter one and there are many proprietary fertilisers for use solely on lawns. As with the application of all feeding and weeding products, it is imperative that the manufacturer's instructions are closely followed, or the lawn may be badly damaged.

Weeding

Lawns which have been correctly laid and properly maintained will be naturally resistant to weed infestation because of the natural growth habit of grasses mentioned in the introduction to this chapter. However, lawns which are not properly maintained are vulnerable to a wide selection of weeds, including creeping buttercup, cat's ear, daisy, dandelion, pearlwort, broad-leaved plantain, clover and yarrow. All these weeds are perennial and will continue to grow unless they are removed or destroyed. In fine lawns, coarse rye-grass would also be considered a weed and would have to be removed.

Wherever possible, the use of chemical weedkillers should be avoided, so any remedy is best undertaken at the first sign of weeds. An old saying, 'Seed for one year, weed for seven', is only too true when it comes to allowing dandelion and other flowering weeds to seed on the lawn. Such plants must be removed by hand as soon as they appear and long before they flower. As their seeds can travel considerable distances in strong winds, an infestation may, unfortunately, start from weeds in a neighbour's garden.

Where chemicals become necessary, spot treatment of isolated weeds is always preferable to spraying or treating large areas. For general use as both a weedkiller and a fertiliser, lawn sand, which comprises three parts sulphate of ammonia, one part sulphate of iron and twenty parts sand, has been very popular for many years and still takes some beating. Applied at a rate of 140g per m² three times a year it will keep down perennial weeds and act as a general fertiliser. With all lawn care, prevention is far better than cure. Therefore, with careful, regular maintenance, including aeration, raking and the application of lawn sand, the lawn will be ready to face even the worst drought.

CHAPTER SIX

The Vegetable Garden

The Master says: 'Good Morning John,
I hope you're feeling nicely,'
The Missus says: 'Your time to start,
Is eight o'clock precisely.'
Why should she always make me feel,
I has to beg her pardon,
Each time she ever shoves her nose,
Inside 'my' kitchen garden.
R. Arkell

I recently read a biography on the great television gardening expert Percy Thrower and was interested to find that he first came to the attention of the media when he was involved in the 'Dig for Victory' campaign following the Second World War. Part of his duties was to show both gardeners and non-gardeners alike how they could produce their own vegetables for the table. I understand that the campaign was very successful and that many families either turned over their garden to growing vegetables or started working on allotments provided by the local councils.

This popularity for home-grown food prevailed until the late 1950s before it started to decline and large areas of allotments going to waste became a common sight. However there has been a renewed interest in home-grown produce recently because of the health scares caused by the over-use of herbicides and pesticides in commercial crop-growing. It is now, once again, becoming popular for the house owner to give up a little of the garden to growing vegetables, or to work an allotment.

For those who are concerned with growing vegetables under drought conditions there are a number of important factors that will be very helpful.

LOCATION OF THE VEGETABLE GARDEN

Most vegetables will only grow well in a light, open, sunny site which is well sheltered from the wind. Where the garden is very exposed, some form of windbreak should be provided that filters the air but does not cast shade. If drainage is poor, it may be improved by adding grit or sharp sand. As cats may be a problem on newly seeded ground, it may be necessary to use some form of deterrent until the plants are established.

PREPARATION OF THE VEGETABLE GARDEN

The main difference between the ornamental garden and the vegetable garden is that, in the latter, plants will only be growing for a relatively short period. Unlike the shrub or tree, which may have a life expectancy of fifty or a hundred years, the life span of a vegetable, such as a potato, onion or leek, is extremely short. This means the soil can be revitalised between crops, which is almost impossible within the ornamental garden.

The preparation of the ground for growing vegetables is described in chapter one and involves double digging and the addition of well-rotted organic material. However, it is important not to dig or walk on the soil when it is wet as this will lead to compaction. To get round this problem, it is becoming more common to develop a system of beds that are each no more than 1.5m wide, which can thus be worked from both sides without ever having to walk on the soil. The bed system is one I advocate for my private house clients as it produces a higher yield, reduces heavy digging and the need for weeding and is ideally suited to automatic irrigation from a rainwater storage system where required. If such a system is adopted, the beds can be raised for ease of maintenance to about 45cm above adjacent ground using old railway sleepers, breeze blocks or even old floorboards. Raised beds, also known as deep beds, are ideal for gardens which have poor, shallow or badly drained soil, and the extra depth of compost may be adapted to suit the specific requirements of particular vegetables.

Choice of Vegetables for Home Growing

In addition to the problem of growing any vegetables while water is restricted, there are a number of other factors which will determine which particular vegetables to grow. Where time or physical ability pose problems, one could choose vegetables such as beetroot, garlic, shallots, leeks, swede, rhubarb, onions and turnips because they require very little attention. If one likes vegetables fresh from the garden and full of taste, then peas, new carrots and sweetcorn are a wise selection. On the other hand, if it is the intention to freeze vegetables, then beans, calabrese and spinach are excellent for this purpose. Many vegetables are quite cheap to purchase at certain times of the year whilst others, because of their short shelf life, are more expensive. By growing some of these more expensive vegetables at home, it is often possible to make considerable savings on the weekly household budget.

Vegetables that are Suitable for Drought Conditions

If one is aware of the water requirements of various vegetables, it is possible, by growing those with the same requirements together, to save wasting large amounts of water.

There are some vegetables that require constant watering during drought conditions. These include runner beans, calabrese, celery, courgettes, lettuce, early potato, spinach, marrows, and tomatoes. In addition, French beans, summer cabbage, cauliflower, peas, sweetcorn and maincrop potato all require watering at key stages in their growth, which may occur during a drought. Vegetables that require very little or no water include beetroot, broccoli, sprouting, Brussels sprouts, spring cabbage, winter cabbage, carrots, winter cauliflower, leeks, onions, parsnips and turnips.

Irrigation Systems for Vegetables

Vegetables, like the majority of plants, take up water through their roots and so it is preferable to provide whatever water is necessary at root level and not onto the surface of the soil. It is possible to use a leaky-pipe watering system as described in chapter two and supply water from a container such as a barrel or tank. If a perforated hose is used, it has the advantage of being easy to move to wherever it is needed. Water no more than twice weekly, making sure the soil around the roots of the plants is thoroughly soaked. Where raised or deep beds are used, the watering system can be built into the initial construction, with flexible hoses which can be placed next to the roots of plants requiring water.

CROP ROTATION

Rotating the types of crops grown in a specific area to avoid the damaging build-up of pests and diseases has been an established practice for many hundreds of years. A three-year system of crop rotation is most common, although it is possible to accommodate a four-year one. For a three-year cycle, divide the vegetable garden into three separate areas. Rotate the growing position of each group of vegetables each year so that it does not return to its original location for three years. The groups of vegetables which may be grown in each particular area are:

Group 1   Peas, Beans
Peas, mangetout, beans, chicory, celery, cucumbers, endives, leeks, spinach, beet, sweetcorn and tomatoes. All these crops require very rich, freshly manured ground.

Group 2   Rootcrop
Beetroot, carrots, parsley, parsnips, salsify, scorzonera, swedes, turnips and potatoes. These crops grow best in well-rotted manure and require a dressing of general fertiliser. It is often a good idea to surround the root crop area with a 50cm-high barrier of plastic or similar material to prevent carrots and parsnips from carrot rootfly attack.

Group 3   Brassicas
Broccoli, Brussels sprouts, cabbages, calabrese, savoys, cauliflower, kohlrabi, swede, turnip, radishes, mustard and kale. As with group 2, all these vegetables require well-rotted manure and a dressing of general fertiliser. It is also common to give the brassica bed a dressing of lime in late winter or early spring.

YEAR ONE	YEAR TWO	YEAR THREE
GROUP 1	**GROUP 3**	**GROUP 2**
VEGETABLES Peas, mange-tout, beans, chicory, celery, cucumbers, endives, leeks, spinach, beet, sweet corn, and tomatoes. SOIL REQUIREMENTS Very rich, freshly manured ground.	VEGETABLES Broccoli, brussels sprouts, cabbages, calabrese, savoys, cauliflower, kohl-rabi, turnip, radishes, mustard, kale. SOIL REQUIREMENTS Requires well rotted manure and a dressing of general fertiliser. Also give the bed a dressing of lime in late winter or early spring.	VEGETABLES Beetroot, carrots, parsley, parsnips, salsify, scorzonera, swedes, turnips, potatoes. SOIL REQUIREMENTS Well rotted manure and dressing with general fertiliser. Provide a 50cm high barrier of plastic to prevent carrot rootfly attack.
GROUP 2	**GROUP 1**	**GROUP 3**
VEGETABLES Beetroot, carrots, parsley, parsnips, salsify, scorzonera, swedes, turnips, potatoes. SOIL REQUIREMENTS Well rotted manure and dressing with general fertiliser. Provide a 50cm high barrier of plastic to prevent carrot rootfly attack.	VEGETABLES Peas, mange-tout, beans, chicory, celery, cucumbers, endives, leeks, spinach, beet, sweet corn, and tomatoes. SOIL REQUIREMENTS Very rich, freshly manured ground.	VEGETABLES Broccoli, brussels sprouts, cabbages, calabrese, savoys, cauliflower, kohl-rabi, turnip, radishes, mustard, kale. SOIL REQUIREMENTS Requires well rotted manure and a dressing of general fertiliser. Also give the bed a dressing of lime in late winter or early spring.
GROUP 3	**GROUP 2**	**GROUP 1**
VEGETABLES Broccoli, brussels sprouts, cabbages, calabrese, savoys, cauliflower, kohl-rabi, turnip, radishes, mustard, kale. SOIL REQUIREMENTS Requires well rotted manure and a dressing of general fertiliser. Also give the bed a dressing of lime in late winter or early spring.	VEGETABLES Beetroot, carrots, parsley, parsnips, salsify, scorzonera, swedes, turnips, potatoes. SOIL REQUIREMENTS Well rotted manure and dressing with general fertiliser. Provide a 50cm high barrier of plastic to prevent carrot rootfly attack.	VEGETABLES Peas, mange-tout, beans, chicory, celery, cucumbers, endives, leeks, spinach, beet, sweet corn, and tomatoes. SOIL REQUIREMENTS Very rich, freshly manured ground.

Fig. 11. Three-year crop rotation scheme

Within the crop rotation system it is possible to grow additional crops, known as catch crops, which are quick-growing and accept most soils. For example, valuable space may be saved by planting catch crops such as lettuce, beetroot and spinach between rows of young Brussels sprouts. It should also be noted that some of the vegetables in the crop rotation system above are not particularly vulnerable to soil-borne pests. These include beetroot, celery, lettuce, marrow, courgettes, spinach and sweet-corn.

GREEN MANURING

Vegetable gardens are ideal places for using green manures, that is, particular plants grown on spare land and then dug in or composted. These plants are especially good for growing through the winter to keep the ground open and prevent loss of nutrients from the soil. Examples are field beans, agricultural lupins, clover, phacelia, trefoil, winter tares, grazing rye, buckwheat, mustard and vetch. However, care must be taken when choosing which green manure to use, as some are not suitable for all vegetables. For instance, mustard is only suitable for brassicas and must not be used for the other groups. Buckwheat, grazing rye and phacelia, though, have been found to be satisfactory for most vegetable groupings.

COMPANION PLANTING WITH VEGETABLES

The concept of growing vegetables with other plants that are beneficial to them has gained in popularity over recent years. However the principle of combining vegetables with herbs and other flowers is far from new and was very much in evidence in the traditional cottage garden. It is recorded as long ago as 1677 that 'there is scarce a cottage in most of the south parts of England but has its proportional garden, so to delight do most men take of it'. These early cottage gardeners must have been aware that some of the common herbs, such as sage, rosemary and mint, not only improved the taste of their meals but were also beneficial to other plants growing beside them.

Because the concept of companion planting is so old it is often difficult to separate fact from folklore. However, below is a list of herbs,

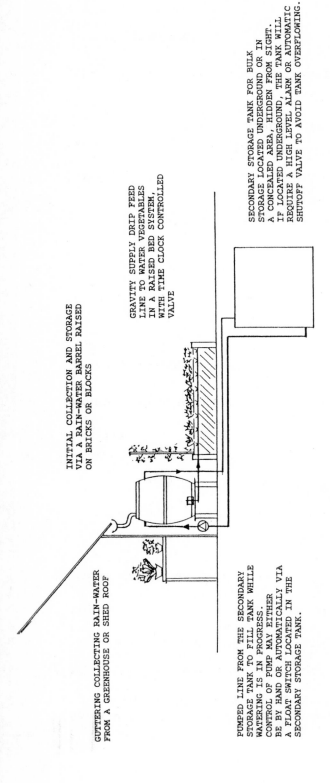

INITIAL COLLECTION AND STORAGE
VIA A RAIN-WATER BARREL RAISED
ON BRICKS OR BLOCKS

GRAVITY SUPPLY DRIP FEED
LINE TO WATER VEGETABLES
IN A RAISED BED SYSTEM,
WITH TIME CLOCK CONTROLLED
VALVE

SECONDARY STORAGE TANK FOR BULK
STORAGE LOCATED UNDERGROUND OR IN
A CONCEALED AREA, HIDDEN FROM SIGHT.
IF LOCATED UNDERGROUND, THE TANK WILL
REQUIRE A HIGH LEVEL ALARM OR AUTOMATIC
SHUTOFF VALVE TO AVOID TANK OVERFLOWING.

GUTTERING COLLECTING RAIN-WATER
FROM A GREENHOUSE OR SHED ROOF

PUMPED LINE FROM THE SECONDARY
STORAGE TANK TO FILL TANK WHILE
WATERING IS IN PROGRESS.
CONTROL OF PUMP MAY EITHER
BE BY HAND OR AUTOMATICALLY VIA
A FLOAT SWITCH LOCATED IN THE
SECONDARY STORAGE TANK.

GRAVITY OVERFLOW SYSTEM TO FEED WATER
INTO THE SECONDARY STORAGE TANK

SCHEMATIC ARRANGEMENT OF A STORAGE WATERING
SYSTEM FOR VEGETABLES PLANTED IN A RAISED BED

Fig. 12. Irrigation system for vegetables

accompanied by the vegetables to which they are generally thought to be beneficial.

Plant	Vegetables benefiting from companion planting
Basil	peppers, tomato, cucumber
Borage	bean
Camomile	broccoli, cabbage, cauliflower
Dill	broccoli, Brussels sprouts, cabbage, cauliflower, cucumber
Hyssop	Brussels sprouts, cabbage, cauliflower
Lupin	corn
Lovage	pepper
Marjoram	pepper
Marigold	bean, potato
Mint	broccoli, Brussels sprouts, cabbage, cauliflower, courgette, marrow, squash
Nasturtium	broccoli, Brussels sprouts, cabbage, cauliflower, courgette, marrow, pumpkin, squash
Parsley	asparagus, tomato
Petunia	potato
Rosemary	broccoli, Brussels sprouts, cabbage, carrot, cauliflower
Sage	broccoli, Brussels sprouts, cabbage, carrot, cauliflower, tomato
Strawberry	bean, lettuce, onion, spinach
Sunflower	melon
Tarragon	aubergine
Thyme	aubergine

There are also a number of vegetables that grow particularly well when planted together. These include: cabbages with celery; tomatoes with beans; carrots with onions; lettuce with cucumbers; potatoes with peas; strawberries with leeks; beans with summer savory; lettuce with radish.

A number of vegetables are also beneficial to other plants. For example, onions and garlic repel many insect pests and black spot on roses; radishes repel flea beetle, and tomatoes control couch grass. It is possible, therefore, within the traditional vegetable garden, to use a variety of plants as 'good companions' to vegetables, and vice versa. This will reduce the need for pesticides and herbicides and provide a much more pleasant and attractive environment for friendly wild-life.

HERBAL SUBSTITUTES FOR PESTICIDES AND HERBICIDES

It is one of the aims of this book to encourage the use of alternative methods of pest control in the garden and there are a number of 'herbal' remedies that can be prepared at home. Soak the leaves of the plants listed below in a bucket of water for up to a week and then spray the liquid produced in the usual way.

To control aphids use nettles and wormwood
To control fleabeetle use elder
To control caterpillar damage to cabbages use tomato
To repel ants use pennyroyals
For general protection against insect pests use garlic

THE ORNAMENTAL VEGETABLE GARDEN

One of the highlights of the 1991 Chelsea Flower Show was 'The Edible Garden', designed and built by staff and inmates of Leyhill Open Prison. Based on circles, the garden illustrated the choices available to the inmates: a fruitless return to crime or a new way forward through growth and change. This was one of the most attractive displays and contained many vegetables which were ornamental in shape, form and colour.

It is possible, within the ordinary domestic garden, to grow vegetables in an ornamental way. Often, the formal bed design, made up of squares, circles or triangles, is most attractive, especially in a relatively small area. Low herb hedges may be used to divide the beds, as can be found in traditional parterres and knot gardens, which is an ideal way to make use of beneficial companion planting, described above. It is also possible to adapt the raised bed system to provide some ornamental features: for example, the rear of the beds may be staked with decorative trelliswork.

Many vegetables, such as ornamental cabbages, lend themselves to the ornamental garden because of their particular shape, form or colour; there are also vegetables that can be grown as presents or to decorate the house. These range from ornamental gourds, which make superb table decorations, to loofahs for the bath or shower.

Choosing Vegetables that are Resistant to Pests and Disease

Much time has been spent by botanists and scientists in recent years in developing vegetables that offer some resistance to the common pests and diseases that occur both in the garden and in commercial horticulture. Although there are still very few vegetables that are totally resistant, much has been accomplished, and the vegetables listed below offer varying degrees of resistance to the pests or disease indicated.

Vegetable	*Disease/pest*	*Varieties Which Show Resistance*
Beetroot	Bolting	Boltardy
Brussels Sprouts	Powdery mildew	Citadel, Mallard, Oliver, Rampart, Troika
Cabbages	Downy mildew	Derby Day, Stonehead
Carrot	Carrot fly	Nandor, Nantucket
Courgettes	Mosaic virus	Supremo
Lettuce	Downy mildew	Avondefiance, Dolly, Musette, Soraya
	Root aphid	Avondefiance, Malika, Musette, Sabine
Parsnip	Canker	Cobham Marrow, Improved Avonresister, White Gem, Gladiator
Potatoes	Blight	Cara, Estima, Maris, Marfona, Peer, Maris Piper, Pentland Dell, Wilja, Kondor
	Common scab	Pentland Javelin, Wilja, Pentland Crown, Arran Pilot
	Mosaic	Cara, Desirée, Maris Bard, Pentland Crown, Romano, Pentland Javelin
	Cyst eelworm	Maris Piper, Pentland Javelin, Cara
Swede	Clubroot	Marian, Chignetto
Tomato	various	Shirley

CHAPTER SEVEN

Garden Care and Maintenance

The cure for this ill is not to sit still,
Or frowst with a book by the fire,
But to take a large hoe and a shovel also
And dig till you gently perspire.
Rudyard Kipling, *I Keep Six Honest Men Serving*

If the garden is to look its best at all times, there are items of care and maintenance that must be done all year round. Obviously, the spring, summer and autumn are more demanding than mid-winter, but even then the garden can suffer from lack of care. It has always been extremely difficult to establish a standard list of monthly garden operations because of the wide variations in climate and garden situation, both in its position in the country and where it sits in relation to the local terrain. Moreover, with the climatic changes we are experiencing at present, even established monthly tasks are having to be rethought. Therefore, great care should be taken when using any form of standard maintenance guide which is based on the average expected conditions at a given time of the year.

The amount of maintenance a garden requires will greatly depend on its style and the type of planting included in it. Here is an approximate guide to the time required for various types of planting. If one takes the work involved in growing and maintaining bedding plants to be the most demanding type of planting (100 per cent), the herbaceous border is 95 per cent, the rock garden is 78 per cent, the mixed border is 74 per cent, the shrub border is 67 per cent and the type of planting which integrates shrubs and trees as described in chapter four, only 15 per cent. In addition to the main planting areas indicated above, lawns, ponds, and garden structures will all require care, and so if time is at a premium, the amount of maintenance needed should be a major consideration when selecting such items as pools, pergolas, fences, gates and summerhouses.

I have made every endeavour in this book to discourage the use of pesticides and herbicides. However, there are several instances where I have suggested the use of relatively 'green' pesticides, such as ICI Rapid, which is friendly to bees, ladybirds and hoverfly larvae. However, if you wish butterflies to feed and lay their eggs in your garden, it must be herbicide and pesticide free for some considerable time.

THE GARDENER'S CALENDAR OF MONTHLY CARE AND MAINTENANCE TASKS

The following calendar provides a basic guide to gardening activities associated with particular times of the year. The items indicated are in no way inclusive and the gardener, in addition to following this guide, should learn the planting, growing and pruning requirements of all trees and plants in his or her garden.

JANUARY

Trees

Remove any dead or diseased branches. Cut back and clean the wounds of any branches that have been broken in storms or from heavy snow. Check all stakes and ties and renew where necessary. If stakes require replacing, take great care not to damage any roots.

Shrubs

Remove any dead or diseased growth or any sections that have been broken by wind or snow. Firm shrubs that have been loosened by wind. Check ties and renew if necessary. In mild weather, well-established, later-flowering shrubs may be pruned back to improve shape and offer less wind resistance. On spring-flowering shrubs, leave this task until after they have flowered.

Annuals and Biennials

Following frosts, check the stability of any biennials planted in the autumn. Firm around plants as necessary. If soil conditions allow, finish preparation of beds for spring sowing of annuals.

Rock Gardens

Check the protection of any plants vulnerable to damage from frost, damp and snow.

Ponds and Pools

If there are icy conditions, check that a hole is maintained in the ice to allow pond gases to escape. DO NOT SMASH ICE ON PONDS WHICH CONTAIN FISH.

Garden Ornaments and Containers

Check all heavy garden ornaments to make sure they are not damaged by frost. Check the condition of any containerised plants.

Roses

Check that no damage has occurred from wind or snow. Firm the ground around any roses that have been loosened by wind. Check stakes and ties and renew if necessary.

The Vegetable Garden

Refrain from treading on any ground that is affected by water or frost.

Fruit

If not yet complete, and weather allowing, complete winter pruning of fruit trees. Dispose of prunings. Feed trees with sulphate of potash.

Lawns

Avoid walking or working on lawns, especially if very wet or frosty. Keep animals off lawns if possible, especially immediately after a thaw. Any late turfing should be completed this month but do not lay turf in frosty conditions. If weather is very wet, take the opportunity to check if there are any particularly soggy areas of lawn that will need future drainage work. Mark such areas either on the ground itself or on a drawing, otherwise you will forget the details when they are required. This is the last month in which to take the mower for overhauling and sharpening if you are to be sure of having it available for the first cut in March.

Garden Structures

Check all garden structures for stability, especially if there has been heavy snow or high winds.

Wildlife

Continue to put out food for birds such as nuts, seeds, meat scraps, old fat, cheese and old fruitcake and, if frosty, ensure plenty of fresh water is available. Do not feed birds dried bread, desiccated coconut or salty foods as these can stick in the bird's crop or cause dehydration.

General

Check the condition of all garden water storage containers, clean them out and wash them through. This is best done when they are full, following a storm, to avoid wasting treated tap water. Repair or replace any leaky taps or pipework connected to containers. During wet conditions, check any connections to rain water gutters and renew or replace as required. Check the lids on all garden water storage containers to ensure a close fit as this will help to keep stored water clean and free of contamination.

This is a good month to repair all garden tools and equipment. When considering ordering plants and seed, avoid plants that will suffer in any future drought, such as begonias, bedding dahlias, fuchsias, pansies and phlox.

February

Trees and Shrubs

Planting of deciduous trees and shrubs may be undertaken if conditions are not frosty or the soil is not too wet. Take the opportunity to work in some well-rotted compost or manure to at least two spades' depth, as this will retain moisture in future. Firm in any trees and shrubs that have been loosened by wind, check stakes and ties and renew if necessary. If not undertaken in the autumn, vigorously cut back shrubs such as buddleias and hydrangeas, which flower on new shoots later in the year.

On beds and borders that are not mulched, scatter dried blood, fish and bone around each plant at a rate of 100g per m^2. Following a long period of rain, mulch the complete bed as described in chapter one. If you live in an exposed location, leave this job until late March.

Now is the time to layer suitable shrubs to increase your stock. Bend a healthy young branch towards the ground, lightly scour its underside and peg down the end into the soil. Check if rooting has taken place in the autumn but do not disturb any young roots for at least a year.

Rock Gardens

Check that all alpines are healthy and protection is satisfactory. Add a mulch of a gritty compost around all plants. In mild areas of the country, alpines may be lifted and divided.

Ponds and Pools

In icy conditions, check that an air space is left in the ice to allow pond gases to escape.

Garden Ornaments and Containers

Check the safety of all heavy garden ornaments that might have been damaged by frost. Check the condition of any containerised plants.

Herbaceous Perennials

In mild areas of the country, lift and divide any herbaceous perennials into plants approximately 10cm across to rejuvenate the plants and increase stock. Give away any unwanted plants or swap for other plants you require. (It is a good idea to get to know other gardeners in your neighbourhood and one way is to become a member of your local gardening society.) Before replanting divided herbaceous perennials, dig in large quantities of organic matter. In more exposed areas of the country, leave this job for a few weeks unless the weather is very mild.

Remove any remaining dead leaves and stems and start to protect the tender new shoots of all herbaceous plants against slug damage. Pick off any slugs, protect each plant with small collars of old carpet and lay down beer traps. Provide support for tall herbaceous plants. Avoid using imported canes; old pea sticks or long twiggy prunings from deciduous hedges and shrubs serve just as well.

Annuals

Lightly fork over any soil prepared in the autumn and mix in blood, fish and bone at a rate of 100g per m². Sow half-hardy annuals in a cold frame or greenhouse towards the end of the month.

Bulbs

Protect crocus and primulas from bird damage. Although a popular method is to tie cotton to small sticks across the beds, I have seen birds badly injured by this practice and think it should be avoided.

Roses

Check that roses are weathering the winter and that no damage has occurred from frost or snow. Check stakes and ties and renew if necessary.

The Vegetable Garden

This is a good time to dig in many of the green manure crops if the soil condition is suitable (i.e. not frozen or too wet). As polythene is not biodegradable, I feel we should discourage its use in the garden, and I am certainly against the purchase of new polythene. However, if you are able to obtain some second-hand, clear polythene or old clear polythene bags, use them to cover seedbeds. This will help to warm and dry the soil, which will bring future crops forward by a few weeks. In the milder areas of the country or in very mild weather it may be possible to begin sowing vegetables outdoors later in the month, but only once the soil temperature at a depth of approximately 7.5cm remains constantly above 7°C. If available, use cloches, which will provide both protection and warmth to developing seeds. Don't forget, when planning the vegetable garden, that some vegetables require far more watering than others (see chapter six). Whilst I am not suggesting that vegetables requiring water should not be planted in the garden, I do feel it is important that such requirements are taken into consideration at the planning stage and that future water storage is included in such plans.

Lift any remaining root vegetables and finish picking Brussels sprouts. If your soil is acid, feed any over-wintering vegetables with nitro-chalk.

Fruit

In mild areas, feed all fruit trees and bushes (except strawberries) with blood, fish and bone at a rate of 150g per m². Protect new buds from bird damage by covering bushes with a 2.5cm mesh net.

Lawns

If the lawn is very wet, avoid walking or working on it. However, if the weather is mild and fairly dry, established lawns may be lightly scarified and a top dressing of compost brushed into the surface. It may be possible to commence preparation work on lawns to be sown, but only if conditions are fairly dry and free of frost.

If you undertake your own lawn mower maintenance, now is the time to do it, ready for a light cut next month. On electric mowers, check all connections, including any extension leads, and ensure you have a functioning residual current circuit breaker (R.C.C.B.). Basic maintenance for a petrol-powered mower includes cleaning the air filter, replacing the engine oil and spark plugs and sharpening the mower blades.

Garden Structures

Repeat last month's check on all garden structures for stability, especially if there have been further snow showers or high winds.

Wildlife

This can be a difficult time for wildlife so take extra care to provide food for birds. Birds attracted into the garden at this time of the year will be tempted to nest in the area and will help you with your pest control in the spring and summer. This is a good time to position new nesting boxes, as they will have a chance to weather, which will make them much more appealing to birds when they start looking for nesting sites. Avoid moving any piles of logs, leaves or similar areas where hedgehogs are hibernating.

General

Check that any watering systems made from buried earthenware pipes and gravel are free to drain. If filled with soil, remove the fill and replace with washed gravel.

This is a good time of the year to start a compost bin. Build a surround which will allow compost to be removed easily and dig over the area within the bin to at least a spade's depth. Site the bin in a semishaded position. The bin can be filled with any waste garden or kitchen material which will rot down. Cover the top of the compost with an old carpet or similar to keep in the heat generated by decomposition.

March

Trees and Shrubs

Any bare-rooted trees or shrubs must be planted by mid-March. Ensure that the roots are in good condition and cut back cleanly any that are broken. Soak them prior to planting and add plenty of well-rotted manure or compost, along with some bone meal, both to the bottom of the planting hole and to the fill material. Any shrubs grown for their decorative stems, such as *Cornus alba* 'Sibirica' and *Rubus cockburnianus*, may be cut back to just above the ground now. However, on those with variegated foliage only cut back a third this year, a third next year and the final third the following year in order to maintain the shrub's shape and attractive leaf colour. Also cut back other winter-flowering shrubs such as *Jasmin nudiflorum* once the flowering period is over.

Rock Gardens

Depending on the weather conditions and exposure, remove protective covers from vulnerable alpines. This may have to be left until April in exposed parts of the country.

Ponds and Pools

This is the time of the year when the pond really starts to come alive with much spawning activity from frogs and toads. Keep the water clear of old leaves and debris but try not to disturb the pond too much at this time.

Herbaceous Perennials

This is a good time to visit garden centres and nurseries to purchase new plants. Remember the need for colour co-ordination in beds and borders and for plants of the right height for each location. When planting, ensure good, well-rotted compost or manure is added to at least one spade's depth to help future water retention. Provide support for potentially tall plants with old, twiggy, pea sticks or deciduous shrub prunings. This is also the last chance to raise and divide overgrown herbaceous perennials. Prune late-flowering clematis back to just above the lowest pair of healthy buds. Lightly trim the stems of summer-flowering clematis back to the highest pair of healthy buds.

Annuals and Biennials

If conditions are suitable, sow hardy annuals outside towards the end of the month. Sow half-hardy annuals in the greenhouse.

Bulbs

Check that all summer-flowering bulbs are firm and free from disease.

Roses

Roses may be pruned in mid-March in mild areas, but this may be best left till mid-April in more exposed areas and locations. Following pruning, apply blood, fish and bone around each plant at a rate of 100g per m² and mulch with well-rotted compost or manure.

The Vegetable Garden

If soil and temperature conditions are suitable, all hardy vegetables, including carrots, lettuce, onions, peas, broad beans, radish and spinach, may be sown now, especially if the soil has been pre-warmed in February as suggested. Brassicas may be started in seed pots for planting out in May. In very mild locations it may be possible to plant out early potato varieties now, but this might be best left until April unless protection can be provided. Prior to planting potatoes, apply Growmore at a rate of 200g per m² and add sulphate of potash at a rate of 20g per m².

Fruit

Finish planting bare-rooted plants. Strawberry beds should be cleaned up and new plants can be planted towards the end of the month in most areas. Feed all fruit trees and bushes with blood, fish and bone at a rate of 200g per m².

Lawns

If the lawn is fairly dry and showing good signs of growth, it may be possible to lightly top the grass but the cut must not be lower than 2.5cm. It is possible however, at this time of the year, for cold winds to discolour newly cut lawns, but these will soon recover. If conditions are dry, the surface of the lawn may be lightly rolled to re-establish any lifting caused by frosts. Begin to hand-pick weeds as soon as possible on established lawns.

Focal points may be so dominant within a garden or landscape that it is essential
to select them with great care.

Garden furniture should always be carefully chosen to suit the site. This formal, white-painted seat seems incongruous in this informal setting.

This narrow, practically unmade path is perfect for an informal woodland walk in a large country garden. The path is in perfect scale with the trees and plants, which have been encouraged to grow wild. The shadows cast by the trees add yet another dimension to the design.

This classical statue is superb for the strictly formal setting in which it is located, but would be totally out of place in a cottage garden setting.

The strictly formal planting of parterres and knot gardens, whilst offering colour, shape and textural interest, is extremely labour-intensive in both planting and maintenance.

The neat box hedges forming squares and rectangles, and the infill of herbaceous plants, establish an atmosphere of formality in this small garden.

As items of hard landscaping represent a high proportion of the cost of the construction of a garden, it is important to ensure that all items included are in harmony with the concept of the design.

These stepping stones have been carefully positioned so as to reflect the line created by the edge of the lawn. The 'line' created adds informality by softening any harsh, formal, straight lines.

The strong, straight line of this clipped hedge at Sizergh Castle acts as a harsh division between the formal and informal parts of the garden.

Some trees, such as these silver birch, show their form all the year round and are often planted for their fine coloured bark.

This group of Delphiniums provides interest in form, texture and colour and would brighten any summer border.

The strong sense of line, created by the planting on the boundary of this croquet lawn, is enhanced by the location of the white painted summer house at the intersection of the two lines.

Even in an informal woodland setting it is important to maintain a sense of balance in planting. If the planting is too dense, without sufficient light and space, it will create an atmosphere of danger and insecurity.

This well-stocked border provides a background of good structural planting with additional seasonal interest provided by shrubs and herbaceous perennials.

Although these beds are newly planted, the careful selection of plants and the relatively close planting give the effect of maturity to the whole garden.

The Judas tree (*Cercis siliquastrum*) forms a fine specimen tree if planted in full sun.

The grass mixture for golf greens and bowling greens is selected to provide the high-quality, dense lawn required.

This Laburnum arch at Kew provides a dazzling display of yellow in late May and early June. However, the Laburnum is not a tree for every garden as it is extremely poisonous.

The Sumach (*Rhus*) forms an attractive specimen tree or focal point and does well in polluted areas.

Wildlife

Keep up feeding birds, although you may be able to reduce the quantities towards the end of the month or in early April, depending on weather conditions. In this way birds will be encouraged to feed on garden pests.

This is the time when frogs and toads start spawning. You may feel that you have too much spawn for your pond, but this will be greatly reduced later if you have fish, as they will eat the tadpoles. If the weather is mild and ornamental fish are becoming active, start feeding them towards the end of the month, but DO NOT OVERFEED.

This may be a good time to think about growing a wild garden. Pick the seeds of flowers that will attract friendly birds and insects into your garden. If you have an informal pool it will provide a fine setting for wild flowers, especially if a small, shallow pool is incorporated where birds can safely bathe.

General

Check the condition of any leaky-pipe watering systems and carry out any repairs or replace.

APRIL

Trees and Shrubs

This is the best time for planting or transplanting evergreen shrubs if not completed in the autumn. Add plenty of organic matter to at least two spades' depth, as well as bone meal. Set up permanent watering points, such as vertical earthenware pipes, around the shrubs so that water is fed to the roots and not wasted on the surface. An alternative is to install a leaky-pipe system to discharge adjacent to the roots (see chapter two). If conditions are dry, ensure newly planted shrubs are kept watered using stored water. Feed beds with blood, fish and bone at a rate of 100g per m². In exposed locations protect newly planted shrubs by erecting a temporary windbreak.

Conifer hedges may be lightly trimmed to shape. Hedges should generally be slightly wider at the bottom than the top so as to shed water and snow and reduce wind resistance. Check the mulch around all shrubs and trees and add as necessary.

Lightly trim winter-flowering heathers to restore desired size and shape. Keep all ornamental beds and borders free of weeds and debris. Remove faded flowers of rhododendrons and mulch with well-rotted compost or manure.

Rock Gardens

This is a good time to purchase and plant alpines. Ensure you provide the correct amount of drainage and mulch around each plant with gritty compost. Divide spring-flowering gentians and saxifrages after flowering.

Ponds and Pools

If the weather in mild, purchase and plant new water lilies and marginals. On established pools, existing lilies and marginals may be removed from their pots and divided with a sharp knife. Replant the best sections in pots with perforated sides, using a clay soil, and cover the surface of the soil with gravel to prevent fish disturbing the roots. Remove any blanket weed. Check that provision is made for amphibians to climb out of the pool easily.

Garden Ornaments and Containers

Check any heavy ornaments and planters to ensure they are safe and secure.

Herbaceous Perennials

In mild areas of the country, chrysanthemums may be planted out towards the end of this month but delay until May in more exposed areas or if there is still a threat from frosts. Provide support for any potentially tall plants.

Annuals and Biennials

Complete sowing of both hardy and half-hardy annuals. Prick out seedlings and move to a cold frame.

Bulbs

Plant summer-flowering bulbs. Dead-head seed pods from early flowering bulbs as flowers begin to fade. Do not remove or tie up the leaves of spring bulbs as this will greatly reduce the vigour of the plant next year.

Roses

Hoe lightly around roses but take care not to damage roots. Begin to check for suckers growing from the base of bushes and as soon as they appear, remove by pulling off from the root. Renew any disturbed mulch. Spray cooled washing-up water onto foliage to deter aphids. If it is absolutely necessary to use chemicals, stick to ICI Rapid, which is friendly to bees, ladybirds and hoverfly larvae. When selecting new roses, choose those that are not susceptible to mildew and blackspot so as to avoid the need to spray.

The Vegetable Garden

Plant onion sets as soon as soil conditions allow. Start sowing catch crops of lettuce, peas and radishes. Sow in small areas that you feel will supply a fortnight's needs. Plant similar amounts at two-week intervals. Plant out any vegetables raised under glass. Begin to plant maincrop potatoes towards the end of the month. Erect barriers against carrot root fly. Place collars made from old sections of carpet around Brassicas. Green manures may be sown at this time for digging in just prior to seeding.

Fruit

Check all fruit tree stakes and ties and loosen if necessary. Cut back raspberries to approximately 15cm from the cane.

Lawns

Increase frequency of mowing for established lawns but do not lower the cut yet. Lawns cut too short now will be less resistant to drought later. In mild areas of the country, treat all lawns with lawn sand at a rate of 140g per m². After approximately ten to twelve days, rake out all thatch and aerate all areas. In more exposed areas of the country, this task should be left till May. Spot repairs may be undertaken either by seeding or turfing, but do not carry out any major seeding projects yet.

Wildlife

Birds will be expending lots of energy from now until after their young have flown the nest and will need lots of food and water. However, birds should be encouraged to feed on garden pests from the end of this month onwards as this will help avoid the use of pesticides in the garden. If birds are nesting in your garden, try to make sure they are as safe as possible from the neighbourhood cats. Other, larger birds, such as magpies, rooks and crows, can also wreak havoc amongst young, smaller birds, but, as this is one of the laws of nature, there is very little one can do to stop it.

General

In newly planted beds and borders, now is the chance to provide a watering system from stored rainwater, either via sunken earthenware pipes filled with gravel or from a leaky-pipe system. In mild parts of the country, hanging baskets may be planted up now. Choose plants that will require least watering as conventional hanging baskets need a great deal of both watering and feeding.

MAY

Trees and Shrubs

Finish dead-heading rhododendrons and azaleas as they complete flowering, but take care not to damage the growing buds. Tie in any new shoots of climbers on fences, trellises or pergolas. Now is a good time to purchase climbers that are in flower, such as early flowering clematis and honeysuckle.

Rock Gardens

Tidy up spring-flowering alpines and check plants are in good condition and free of pests. Soil may be added to new rock gardens if the levels have subsided. Remove any debris from around plants and renew mulch if required.

Ponds and Pools

Remove and divide water lilies and marginals if not done in April. Keep the surface of the pool clean and continue feeding fish if natural food is not available. This is a good time to introduce new fish into the pond. They usually arrive from the supplier in a plastic bag containing some of the water they have been used to. The complete bag should be lowered into the pond and left for up to half an hour so that the water temperature in the bag slowly adjusts to that of the pool. They may then be released.

Containers

Plant up containers using good, fine compost. Do not use ordinary garden soil as it is unsuitable for containers. Start a watering programme to ensure the compost does not dry out. Avoid wasting water by watering at root level and preventing too much water draining away.

Herbaceous Perennials

Herbaceous plants may be sown outside towards the end of the month if the weather is mild. In exposed locations, or if the weather is cold, leave until early or mid-June. Cut back any early flowering herbaceous perennials to encourage another flush of flower.

Annuals and Biennials

Harden off all plants grown under glass for two weeks and then plant out when the soil is warm enough and there is no risk of damage from frost. Sow biennials such as forget-me-nots, polyanthus, sweet williams, hollyhocks and wallflowers in a nursery bed towards the end of the month. Leave this job until mid-June in more exposed areas.

Bulbs

Complete dead-heading of tulips and daffodils. If you wish to remove spring-flowering bulbs, now is the time to do it, but let the foliage die back first. Ornamental tulips should be lifted and dried, ready for replanting in the autumn.

Roses

Continue to spray roses with cold washing-up water.

Vegetable Garden

Continue sowing autumn and winter vegetables. Provide support for peas. Earth up potatoes as soon as shoots appear. In mild areas of the country, tender vegetables may be planted now. In more exposed areas, leave until early June.

Fruit

Net strawberry plants against damage from birds. Thin out raspberry canes. Mulch around fruit bushes with well-rotted garden compost to keep down evaporation of water from the soil.

Lawns

In mild regions of the country, new lawns may be sown this month. On established lawns, lightly rake the lawn prior to mowing. If growing conditions are good, slightly lower the cut but still keep it as high as possible in order to prepare the lawn for any later drought conditions. Where a new, seeded lawn is planned and if no prior preparation has yet been undertaken, start cultivating the ground for sowing at the end of August.

To Avoid Pests Without Using Chemicals

If the previous winter has been mild and aphids have not been killed off, now is the time when they will cause most harm to roses, honeysuckles and young shrubs and trees. Use cold washing-up water as a spray both to destroy aphids and remove sooty mould, which will often occur when aphids are numerous. If it is absolutely necessary to use chemicals, stick to ICI Rapid, but do not spray it on soft fruit, melon or cucumber. Make a habit of checking all growing plants for slugs and caterpillars, pick off and destroy them.

Wildlife

Continue to feed birds only if natural supplies of food are not available.

General

Ensure that as much rainwater as possible is collected during this month in preparation for any future drought. Concentrate on watering newly planted trees, shrubs and herbaceous plants and vegetables, but take care not to waste water.

JUNE

Trees and Shrubs

Very little work is required on trees and shrubs this month. However, continue to check for damage and renew mulch where required. Water newly planted trees and shrubs using a permanent watering system so that the lower roots are encouraged to extend deep into the ground and not grow up towards the surface of the soil. Trim hedges.

Rock Gardens

Continue to remove any debris and tidy plants. Alpines may be propagated this month from cuttings.

Ponds and Pools

Continue to feed fish if natural supply is insufficient. Remove fading flowers of irises, etc. If plants have grown very large, trim back some of the foliage to reduce wind resistance. Check no damage has been done to aquatic plants by fish. Make good the gravel mulch on the surface of the soil in pots if necessary.

Garden Ornaments and Containers

Continue to water and feed all containers, window boxes and hanging baskets.

Herbaceous Perennials

Dead-head all flowers as they fade. Provide any necessary support for tall plants. Trim any herbs that look straggly. Divide polyanthus and primulas after flowering and plant in a nursery bed until the autumn. Sow herbaceous perennials in seedbeds as soon as possible, ready for flowering next year.

Bulbs

Tidy up dead foliage of naturalised spring-flowering bulbs once they have died down. Brush well-rotted compost into the area to encourage healthy lawn growth.

Annuals and Biennials

Sow biennials such as forget-me-nots, polyanthus, foxgloves and wallflowers. Protect the seeded areas from being disturbed by birds or cats. Complete bedding displays.

Roses

Continue spray treatment against aphids. Dead-head all roses as they fade, to encourage further blooms.

The Vegetable Garden

Check Brassicas for damage from caterpillars, remove and destroy by hand. Ensure the soil is moist around french beans, runner beans, celery, courgettes, cucumbers and marrows, and retain the moisture by mulching with well-rotted compost. Continue to earth up potatoes and sow hardy vegetables.

Fruit

Remove any dead or damaged wood from plum trees. Protect soft fruit from damage by birds if you have not already done so. Trim the runners on summer-fruiting strawberries.

Lawns

The foliage of any bulbs naturalised in the grass may be removed now. Rake the lawn regularly before mowing as this will reduce future weed problems. If there are drought conditions, refrain from cutting the lawn until really necessary and even then keep the cut as high as possible. If there is no drought, mow lawns at least once a week but, unless the lawn is ornamental, keep the cut as long as possible to prepare the lawn for any drought in the next few months. Also spike the lawn at least once this month to ensure any rainwater reaches the roots easily. Continue preparation of proposed new areas of lawn, ready for seeding at the end of August.

Problems Caused by Weeds from Neighbouring Gardens

As weed seeds may be blown a considerable distance, the weeds from neighbouring gardens may root in yours. If your soil is properly mulched, developing weeds may be easily removed by pulling out and composting.

Where there is a problem with creeping weeds, such as ground elder and bindweed, from next-door gardens, ensure that weeds on your side of the fence are regularly removed so that they do not have a chance to establish. It is possible to present a barrier to such creeping weeds by sinking old plastic bags vertically into the soil to a depth of at least 20cm. This will not provide total protection but it will make management on your side of the fence much easier.

JULY

Trees and Shrubs

If there is a drought, now is the time when you will see the benefit of all your hard work in preparing for such a condition. Concentrate any watering on newly planted shrubs and trees and ensure the mulch is intact. Continue to tie in the new growth of climbers.

Rock Gardens

Continue to take cuttings from alpines.

Ponds and Pools

If the weather is hot, make sure oxygen and water levels are maintained. Overgrown aquatic plants and marginals may be divided.

Garden Ornaments and Containers

Continue watering containers, window boxes and hanging baskets.

Herbaceous Perennials

Lift and divide irises. Dead-head flowers as they fade. Sow new herbaceous perennials outdoors in a nursery bed for transplanting in early autumn.

Annuals and Biennials

Finish sowing biennials such as forget-me-nots, polyanthus, foxgloves and wallflowers. Protect the seeded areas from birds and cats. Dead-head flowers as they fade.

Bulbs

Plant autumn-flowering bulbs such as crocus and cyclamen.

Roses

Check condition of all roses. Continue to spray with cooled washing-up water. Remove all suckers by pulling off at the root. Continue to dead-head as flowers fade.

The Vegetable Garden

Pick beans and peas regularly to encourage replacement growth. Check for blackfly. Spray off or use ICI Rapid if absolutely necessary. Pinch out the tops of runner beans as they reach the top of the supports. Control cabbage white caterpillar by picking off and destroying by hand. Plant out autumn and winter cauliflower and cabbage. Sow spring cabbage towards the end of the month in mild regions of the country. Leave until August in more exposed areas.

Fruit

Start to pick blackcurrants approximately two weeks after they have turned black. Prune back by one-third the most heavily laden branches. Also remove broken or weak growths. Prune gooseberries, and red and white currants. Peg down summer-fruiting strawberries.

Lawns

If there are drought conditions, do not cut the lawn until really necessary and even then keep the cut as high as possible. The lawn colour may be spoilt a little from lack of water but if it has been properly prepared and cared for as described in chapter five, it should quickly recover following the first good shower of rain. Continue preparation of proposed new areas of lawn ready for seeding at the end of August.

Garden Structures

Now is a good time to undertake any maintenance or redecoration of garden structures. Take care that any wood preservative used in the garden is safe to plants, animals, insects and birds. When selecting colours, choose the 'earth' colours that are sympathetic to adjacent plants and trees.

Paving and Walling

Construct or repair areas of paving and walls, making sure any new building is given adequate foundations. Ensure any materials used will complement the overall style of the garden.

Wildlife

Trim the grass in the wild garden to restrict the growth of vigorous weeds, which will take over if left alone. Take care that wild animals such as hedgehogs and grass snakes are safe before undertaking this job.

AUGUST

Trees and Shrubs

August is a good month to trim shrubs and hedges, such as laurel, holly, hornbeam, box, yew, beech and privet, so that any new growth has a chance to harden off before the winter. Give evergreen conifer hedges, such as Leyland cypress, a final trim towards the end of the month. Concentrate on watering newly planted trees and shrubs with the permanent watering system. If you are going on holiday or leaving the garden for some time, especially in conditions of drought, try to make sure that anyone who looks after your newly planted trees and shrubs or other vulnerable plants uses stored rather than tap water.

Take semi-ripe cuttings from shrubs such as box, ceanothus, cytisus, escallonia, euonymus, hydrangea, hypericum and philadelphus. Prune summer-flowering shrubs.

Ponds and Pools

Remove blanket weed but place it close to the pool for a few days to give any creatures hiding in it a chance to return to the pool. Compost the weed. Plant new aquatic plants if not done before. Tidy up existing plants and remove any weed. If the weather is hot, make sure oxygen and water levels are maintained.

Containers

Continue to water all containers at least once a day at the roots. Feed twice a week with liquid fertiliser made from manure.

Herbaceous Perennials

Continue dead-heading as necessary. Collect seedheads for future planting. Store in paper bags and mark clearly with the plant name.

This is a good time of the year to check any spaces and make plans to redesign the herbaceous border for next year.

Annuals and Biennials

Pinch out the tips of wallflowers to stop them becoming too leggy. Sow hardy annuals such as alyssum, calandulas, candytuft, clarkia, godetia, larkspur and nigella in late August or early September.

Bulbs

If the soil conditions are suitable, bulbs such as daffodils, colchicums, winter aconites and crocus may be planted from this month onwards.

Roses

Continue dead-heading and remove any vigorous, upright shoots that will affect the shape of the plant. Prune rambler roses when the flowering period is over. This is a good time to order new roses for autumn delivery.

The Vegetable Garden

Prepare shallots for lifting by severing roots once the foliage starts to turn yellow. Continue to pick beans and courgettes to keep up level of cropping. Lift beetroot when they are a good size but not too large. Trim herbs such as mint, chives and marjoram to encourage new growth. Sow spring cabbage as weather conditions allow, depending on the region. In regions liable to early frosts, sow turnips to use the tops for spring greens.

Fruit

In mild regions of the country, prune restricted and dwarf forms of apple and pears such as cordons and espaliers. Leave this job until the end of August or beginning of September in less exposed regions of the country. Cut back fruited shoots on wall-trained peach trees and tie in new shoots. Protect ripening blackberries and autumn raspberries from bird damage. Clear away old foliage from strawberries once fruiting is finished. Remove fruited and weak raspberry canes and tie in new ones.

Lawns

Do not treat lawns after the end of July. Continue to mow in order to maintain appearance, unless there are drought conditions, when you should refrain from mowing if at all possible.

Wildlife

In conditions of drought, when water may be difficult to find, provide water for birds and animals. Make sure it is clean and position it so that birds are not endangered by cats when drinking or bathing.

SEPTEMBER

Trees and Shrubs

Newly planted evergreen trees and shrubs may require some protection from winds from this month onwards. Take semi-ripe cuttings from shrubs and trees.

Ponds and Pools

Cover small ponds with a framed wire mesh to prevent ingress of autumn leaves. Keep feeding fish and change to a high-protein diet to build them up for the winter.

Garden Ornaments and Containers

Maintain watering and feeding programme as necessary. Move containers with tender plants under cover.

Herbaceous Perennials

Now is a suitable time to plant out young herbaceous perennials whilst many of the established plants are still in leaf. Ensure that the area is carefully prepared and, in particular, that plenty of organic material is dug well in prior to planting. Take cuttings of tender plants such as pelargoniums prior to lifting and storing next month.

Annuals and Biennials

Plant out sweet williams, wallflowers and forget-me-nots over the next month, dependent on weather conditions. Tidy up planting areas and any straggly plants.

Bulbs

Bulbs such as daffodils, cyclamen, colchicums, winter aconites and crocus may be planted from this month onwards. Now is the time to naturalise bulbs in grass by planting them in groups or drifts under the turf. Make sure they have drainage by sifting a little coarse sand into the bottom of the planting hole.

Roses

Continue dead-heading. Trim back any long stems to a third of the original length, except for roses which have ornamental hips, which should be left.

The Vegetable Garden

Transplant spring cabbage. Sow turnips early in the month to use the tops for spring greens.

Fruit

Pick apples and pears as they ripen and store in a cool, frost-free place. Cut down old blackberry and loganberry canes following fruiting and tie in new shoots.

Lawns

Rake out thatch this month and aerate compacted areas. Prepare and reseed any bare areas and protect from bird damage.

OCTOBER

Trees and Shrubs

Take hardwood cuttings of deciduous trees and shrubs once leaves have fallen. Check, and renew where necessary, the mulch around all trees and shrubs, which will protect the roots from frosts. Start planting deciduous trees and shrubs as soon as the leaves have fallen. Make sure you add organic matter to at least two spades' depth. Support trees and shrubs where necessary with stakes and ties.

Rock Gardens

Some alpines, especially those with silver or hairy leaves, may require protecting from this month onwards, especially if conditions are wet. Use glass or clear rigid plastic on wire supports. Remove any fallen leaves from alpines as these may damage plants.

Ponds and Pools

Remove and check submerged pumps for winter storage. Keep feeding fish with a high-protein diet such as ants' eggs, but stop when weather turns cold and fish become less active.

Herbaceous Perennials

Now may be a good time to lift and divide herbaceous perennials whilst they are still in leaf. Lift plants and divide with two forks placed back to back. Replant those sections that are approximately 10cm in diameter.

Give away or swap any plants left over. Lift tender plants such as pelargoniums for winter storage.

Annuals

Sow hardy annuals such as candytuft, clarkia, cornflower, larkspur, nigella and scabious thinly in rows and protect with cloches. Transplant to final location in spring. Make a note of the success of annual planting and plan any revisions for next year. Clear beds of any annuals hit by frosts.

Bulbs

Plant hyacinths, irises and lilies later this month. Lift tender bulbs, such as begonias and gladioli, before first frosts threaten. Plant tulips towards the end of the month if conditions are suitable.

Roses

Continue dead-heading. Trim back any long stems to a third of the original length to reduce wind resistance in winter.

The Vegetable Garden

Lift maincrop or late potatoes when the haulms die down. Store healthy tubers in a cool, dark, frost-free place in thick paper sacks. Finish picking tomatoes before first frosts. Lift beetroot and pick marrows towards the end of the month but prior to first frosts. Complete harvesting of runner beans.

Fruit

Complete picking of any apples and pears not done last month and store in a cool, frost-free place. Cut down remaining blackberry and loganberry canes following fruiting and tie in new shoots.

Lawns

Sweep up fallen leaves and lightly rake the lawn. If weather conditions are suitable and the lawn is still growing, lightly mow the lawn with the blades set high.

Garden Structures

As October has been quite windy over recent years, now is a good time to check all garden structures. Carry out any repairs required immediately as garden structures such pergolas and summerhouses can be extremely dangerous in strong winds.

Containers

The root systems of some plants in exposed containers, which cannot be taken indoors, may require protecting from frosts from this month onwards by wrapping the container in straw or similar material.

Wildlife

Start to feed birds now if you intend to attract them into your garden all winter. However, only feed them now if you intend to continue the feeding *all* winter as you may be distracting them from other, longer-lasting sources of food. Feed with nuts, seeds, cooked meat scraps, old fat, cheese and old fruit cake. Avoid dried bread, desiccated coconut or salty food. Also make sure birds and animals in your garden have plenty of fresh water. Construct several 'wild' areas, such as piles of leaves and twigs, which will remain undisturbed all winter. These will provide a safe place for hibernating hedgehogs.

NOVEMBER

Trees and Shrubs

This is the time to protect any newly planted conifers, evergreens or other vulnerable trees and shrubs. Hessian or old sacking fixed to stakes driven into the ground is most suitable and looks far more attractive than black plastic. Smaller plants which are vulnerable to frost or wind damage may be covered over with straw or sacking if some form of frame is provided as a support. Ensure the root systems of shrubs are protected from frost by checking the mulch. Add or replace as necessary. Continue to take deciduous hardwood cuttings from trees and shrubs such as cornus, philadelphus and weigela. Prune any dead or diseased wood from trees and shrubs. Do not paint the wounds, but make sure the cut is clean by trimming with a knife.

Bare-rooted trees and shrubs may be planted now in frost-free conditions. Soak the roots for two or three hours prior to planting. Ensure plenty of rich organic matter is added to the ground as described in chapter one. If you are not able to plant immediately, heel-in the tree or shrub in the vegetable garden until ready to plant.

Check the stakes and ties on all trees and shrubs. Repair or replace as necessary. Trim back the summer growth of wisteria to two buds from the main stem. Remove short shoots and tie in healthy stems for next year's growth. Tie up any conifers that may be damaged by snow.

Rock Gardens

Check protection of alpines. Trim and tidy late-flowering alpines and collect seed. Clear away any dead leaves and debris. Renew any disturbed chippings or mulch.

Ponds and Pools

Clear out any dead leaves and debris. Remove any tender pond plants to a frost-free place but do not forget to keep the soil moist.

Garden Ornaments and Containers

Make sure that all ornaments and containers that are to remain outside for the winter are safe and secure. Provide protection where necessary.

Herbaceous Perennials and Grasses

Cut down tall ornamental grasses to within approximately 10cm of the ground, but leave pampas and miscanthus. Tidy up any remaining top growth of perennials and take seed. Protect parsley, chives and mint to prolong cropping.

Annuals

Cover the over-wintering seedlings of hardy annuals with cloches during cold conditions.

Lawns

Continue to sweep up fallen leaves and lightly rake the lawn. If the weather is very mild it may still be necessary to mow the lawn with the blades set high, but if conditions are very wet it is best to keep off the lawn altogether. It is still possible to lay turf on prepared ground if conditions are not too cold or wet.

Once mowing is finished for the year, take the mower to be serviced so that it is ready for the first cut next year. For a petrol mower, most mechanics will undertake a complete overhaul, including cleaning the air filter, replacing the engine oil and spark plugs, checking the carburettor, sharpening the blades and painting any surfaces liable to rust. If you intend to do your own lawn mower maintenance early next year, clean and grease all bare parts and empty the mower of petrol.

Bulbs

Feed naturalised bulbs as soon as they come into leaf by top dressing with well-rotted compost and brushing into the lawn. Plant tulips early in the month if conditions are suitable.

Roses

Take hardwood cuttings from roses now. Prune repeat-flowering, climbing roses by cutting back all new growth by one third. Cut back any remaining long stems on rose bushes to reduce wind resistance but leave hard pruning until the spring.

The Vegetable Garden

Complete harvesting of all crops this month, including beetroot, as conditions may be very unfavourable next month. Clear ground, remove any debris from the area and prepare the ground for winter by digging over and mixing in plenty of organic material. Prepare bean trenches for next year. Dig a trench 80cm wide by 30cm deep and fill to within 10cm of the top with garden and kitchen waste before topping off with good soil. Remove any dying leaves from over-wintering brassicas to minimise disease next year.

Fruit

Prune blackcurrants if not done before. Remove the nets from fruit cages or damage may occur from a build-up of snow. If necessary, the close-mesh netting may be replaced with a 10cm mesh net to protect fruit bushes from damage by pigeons. Plant bare-rooted fruit trees, incorporating plenty of organic matter at the roots. Check stored fruit for any signs of deterioration. Prune free-standing apple and pear trees to produce an open shape. Remove any broken or diseased branches and trim the wound with a knife. Avoid any damage to plum, peach or cherry trees, as this may leave them vulnerable to silver leaf infection.

Wildlife

Put out food for birds and make sure both birds and animals have plenty of fresh water, especially in frosty conditions. Now is the time to clear the wild flower area, but take care not to disturb any hibernating or over-wintering wildlife.

General

Leaves should be collected and stored in old plastic bags for up to two years to make leaf mould. All other suitable garden waste should be composted.

Once all major gardening tasks are finished for the year, now is the best time to clean and oil all garden tools and equipment. Any repairs to tools and equipment should also be undertaken now.

DECEMBER

Trees and Shrubs

Deciduous shrubs may be cut back now to improve the general shape. In snowy conditions, gently shake snow from trees and shrubs to avoid damage to branches. It is better to remove snow from branches as the possibility of damage is increased if the snow turns to ice. This is especially important for conifers, which may be permanently distorted by snow damage. Continue to check the stakes and ties on all trees and shrubs. Repair or replace as necessary.

Bulbs

If the ground conditions are not too wet or frozen, it is still possible to plant tulips early in the month.

Roses

Check stakes and ties on all roses and repair or replace as necessary.

The Vegetable Garden

Turnips should be raised at the end of the month. Now is a good time to establish the cropping plan for next year. Do not forget the need to rotate crops as detailed in chapter six.

Ponds and Pools

In freezing conditions it is imperative that a space is left in the ice to allow the release of gases which, if trapped in the pond, can be harmful to fish and create a pressure build-up. Leave a ball floating on the pond, as this will help reduce ice build-up and will also act as a pressure release.

Fruit

Check condition of stored fruit.

Rock Garden

Check the protection of alpines. Continue to clear away any debris. Check and renew mulch or stones.

Lawns

Remove any dead leaves or other debris but keep off lawns in wet or frosty conditions.

Garden Structures

Now is a good time to repair any fences and trellises because many climbers and wall shrubs are dormant.

Wildlife

Continue to feed birds. It is very important now that all birds and animals have plenty of fresh water, especially in frosty conditions. This is also a good time to clean out and reline old nesting boxes.

General

This is a good time of the year to take a look at the overall design of your garden and to plan any changes. In December, the basic structure of the garden may be clearly seen. As all deciduous shrubs and trees are without leaf and there are no annuals and herbaceous perennials, it is the basic line and shape of your garden that is presented. Take photographs and make notes and sketches of any areas that you feel could be improved. Part of the pleasure for a gardener in December and January is to sit snug and warm indoors by the fire and plan the glory of next year's garden.

CHAPTER EIGHT

Wildlife in the Garden

I value my garden more for being full of blackbirds than of cherries, and very frankly give them fruit for their songs.
Joseph Addison

We may spend an inordinate time and large quantities of money designing, constructing and planting the area around our homes but, without wildlife, it would not truly be a garden. The singing of birds, the drone of bees and the erratic flight of multicoloured butterflies are all an integral part of the atmosphere of the garden. In addition, there are many birds, animals and insects which are beneficial to our gardens and may be considered the gardener's 'friends'. By learning a little of the ways of these creatures we can attract them into our garden and make their lives, which are sometimes very short, as pleasant as possible.

Except for wildlife that prefer humid conditions, such as frogs and toads, there are many forms of wildlife that will live in, or visit a garden that is designed to thrive well on drought conditions.

BIRDS

Birds are an important part of any garden and one that is devoid of birdsong is a very sorry place. During the nesting season, birds can be a great help to the gardener in reducing the population of garden pests such as slugs and caterpillars.

The types of birds you may see in a garden will depend greatly on the area in which you live. However, as they are extremely adaptable, there are many birds that will make their home even in a busy, noisy city.

If the correct food is put out regularly, many species of bird will be attracted to your garden. Suitable foods include fat, suet, cereals, fresh nuts, sultanas or raisins, cheese, bread crumbs (if soaked in water first) and bacon cut into short lengths. Avoid salted peanuts, desiccated coconut, dried bread, uncooked meat and any spicy food.

By placing a well-designed bird table, as detailed in figure 13, in a safe place that can be seen from the house, feeding birds can provide constant delight most of the year. However, birds should be encouraged to feed on natural foods, such as garden pests and berries, once they are available. Many fine trees and shrubs may be grown in the garden which will attract birds and other wildlife. These include Pyracantha, Sambucus, Ilex, Cotoneaster, Crataegus and Berberis.

Some birds are extremely territorial whilst others live and eat in large groups. Robins, for example, will fiercely defend what they consider to be their own territory; starlings, however, seem to thrive in squabbling, bustling hordes.

There has been relentless destruction of the natural nesting places of birds over the last fifty years. For instance, it is estimated that 240,000km of Britain's hedgerows have been destroyed since the Second World War. In addition, the two severe storms in 1987 and 1990 destroyed many large, old trees, which provided nesting sites for many species. By providing substitutes in the form of nesting boxes it is possible to attract birds into the garden. Boxes should be placed so that they are as protected as possible from the neighbourhood cats or the occasional squirrel. Different types of box are taken up by different species of bird, so it is worth giving some thought to which birds you wish to attract before erecting suitable homes for them. Birds which will nest in a garden, given the correct conditions, include the robin, tits, nuthatches, thrushes, blackbirds, house martins and swallows. Magpies will also nest in the garden but, as they can attack the young of smaller birds, you may wish to discourage them.

LADYBIRDS

The name ladybird, ladybug or ladybeetle derives from 'beetle of Our Lady', a name given to this small insect during the Middle Ages. There

Fig. 13 A bird table

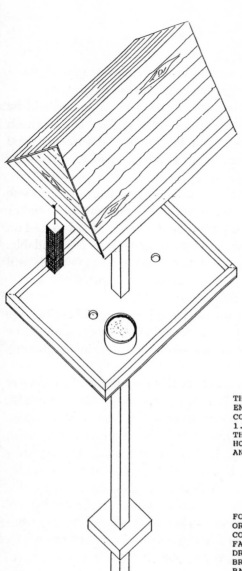

THE BIRD TABLE SHOULD BE STRONG
ENOUGH TO WITHSTAND ALL WEATHER
CONDITIONS AND BE APPROXIMATELY
1.7M TALL. A ROOF WILL HELP KEEP
THE FOOD DRY AND TWO OR THREE
HOLES IN THE PLATFORM WILL HELP
ANY SPILT WATER TO DRAIN AWAY.

FOOD MAY BE LAID ONTO THE PLATFORM
OR HELD IN PLASTIC COATED WIRE CAGE
CONTAINERS. SUITABLE FOOD INCLUDES
FAT, SUET, CEREALS, FRESH NUTS,
DRIED FRUIT, CHEESE, WHOLEMEAL
BREADCRUMBS AND SHORT LENGTHS OF
BACON. ALSO PROVIDE PLENTY OF
FRESH WATER, ESPECIALLY IN FROSTY
CONDITIONS.

AN ADJUSTABLE, INVERTED WOODEN BOX
WILL HELP STOP SQUIRRELS AND CATS
FROM REACHING THE BIRD TABLE.

PLACE THE BIRD TABLE IN AN OPEN
POSITION WHERE BIRDS WILL FEEL
SAFE FROM ATTACK BY THE NEIGHBOUR-
HOOD CATS.

are forty-five different species to be found in Britain and, as both the adult and its larvae are voracious eaters of aphids, sometimes working their way through as many as one hundred in a single day, they may be considered some of the gardener's best friends and should be protected at all times.

The most common ladybird is the red, seven-spot variety, which is to be found almost everywhere; but the two-spot and ten-spot types are also fairly common. All are carnivorous except for the twenty-four spot ladybird, which feeds on clover leaves. The insect's interesting colouring has developed to warn would-be predators that it is unpleasant to eat. As a further deterrent, the ladybird also gives off a horrible, orange-coloured, pungent liquid, actually blood, when attacked or disturbed.

Ladybirds like to over-winter in secluded, protected places such as beneath the bark of trees, or in cracks in the walls of outbuildings. The population explosion of 1976, which by July of that year had reached between 200 and 300 times its normal level, was caused by the warm summers of the previous two years. Although such increases have been comparatively rare in the past, they may become more common in the future if climatic conditions continue to change. Fortunately, as the weather conditions which favour ladybirds also have the effect of increasing the numbers of aphids, there will be plenty of food for the hungry insects and less work in spraying for the gardener.

BATS

For the uninitiated, bats can be frightening creatures. However, their reputation for drinking blood, or any other grisly attributes, are wholly unfounded. The bats one may see flying around at dusk feed on nothing more exotic than small insects, caddisflies, beetles and moths.

Bats have adapted well to living amongst human beings and may be found roosting in lofts, behind hanging tiles or drainpipes and within the soffit of the roofs of houses in both the town and country. During the summer they also form nursery roosts of up to one hundred bats in places such as barns and church spires.

Bats are now protected by law and are slowly becoming accepted for the lovely little animals they are. Their flitting and darting style of flight at dusk is most exciting to watch and their reputation for becoming tangled in your hair is greatly exaggerated.

BUTTERFLIES

One of the most pleasant aspects of the summer garden is the sight of feeding butterflies, flitting from plant to plant. Although there are fifty-eight species of butterfly that may be seen in Great Britain, some of these are now extremely rare and there are only about a dozen which are commonly found in the garden. These include the red admiral, whites, comma, common blue, holly blue, peacock and painted lady.

Butterflies may be attracted into your garden to feed by growing nectar-producing plants. These include aubretia, buddleia, snowdrop, crocus, honesty, sweet william, hebe, forget-me-not, lilac, lavender, thyme, privet, phlox, golden rod, michaelmas daisy and the ice plant, *Sedum spectabile*. If it is possible to dedicate an area of the garden to wild flowers, these may include lady's smock, thistles, honeysuckle, primrose, brambles, clover and stinging nettles, all of which provide nectar for various species of butterfly.

It is far more difficult to create a garden in which butterflies will breed. First, the garden must be absolutely free of all pesticides and herbicides. Second, the correct food plants must be provided for caterpillars and these may differ from the nectar plants to attract adult butterflies. Holly blues and large and small whites are probably the easiest to encourage and it is well worth trying.

HONEY BEES

One of the first insects to appear in the garden as the weather starts to warm up in late spring is the honey bee. Through the ages, man has kept bees for their supply of honey. In the garden, however, it is their work of pollination for which the gardener must be most grateful.

Honey bees live in colonies which sometimes contain more than 60,000 or 70,000 insects. Each colony revolves around one fertilised female, the queen, and all other bees are her offspring. Apart from her initial fertilisation flight, the queen remains in her nest all her life and her sole duty is to lay eggs. Her egg-laying capacity is incredible, sometimes numbering up to 1,000 eggs a day. The majority of bees within any colony are female, known as workers, but there will also be a very small percentage of males, the drones, during spring and summer, which are held in reserve for fertilising a new queen if the existing queen is ageing or deteriorating.

The proportion of workers to drones, the selection of a new queen and the smooth running of the colony is controlled by chemical 'messages', pheromones, which are produced in the mouth parts of the bees themselves. Initiating from the queen and other members of the colony, the pheromones are distributed as the workers feed and lick the queen's mouth. When those bees feed other workers, and also the developing larvae, the 'message' is passed to every member of the colony.

There are different pheromones for every major function within the colony, but probably the most important is that produced when the queen is coming to the end of her useful life. At this time there is a decline in her production of a pheromone known as 'queen substance' and when this is communicated throughout the colony, the workers begin to feed up another female to take her place.

One of the most interesting aspects of communication within the bee colony occurs when a bee has discovered a particularly fine source of nectar. If the source is within approximately 90m she will undertake what is known as a 'round dance', rotating both clockwise and anticlockwise. As the rate and vigour of the dance indicates the richness of the source, it is particularly hypnotising to see the returning bee if an extremely rich source of nectar has been discovered. If the source is over 90m away, the bee undertakes a figure of eight dance, interspersed with several 'runs' in the direction of the find. The length of the runs and the number of 'wriggles' indicate to other workers the approximate distance of the source of the nectar.

Bees may be attracted to your garden by growing appropriate food plants. In Britain, clover and lime flowers between them provide 95 per cent of the honey crop. However, heathers, the pollen from apple, pear, plum and cherry trees, dandelion, oil rape seed, blackberry, broad bean and hawthorn all provide food for bees. For the ornamental garden, plants such as *Aubretia, Echinops, Crocus, Eranthus, Saxifraga, Limnanthus, Melissa, Origanum, Lavandula, Salvia, Ulex, Borago, Hyssopus, Lythrum, Nepeta, Phacelia* and *Rosmarinus* all attract bees and can be incorporated into even the most formal arrangement.

The drone of honey bees at work is one of the most pleasant sounds of summer and the gardener should do everything possible to protect them from harm by avoiding the use of pesticides and herbicides and by encouraging neighbours, friends and family to do the same.

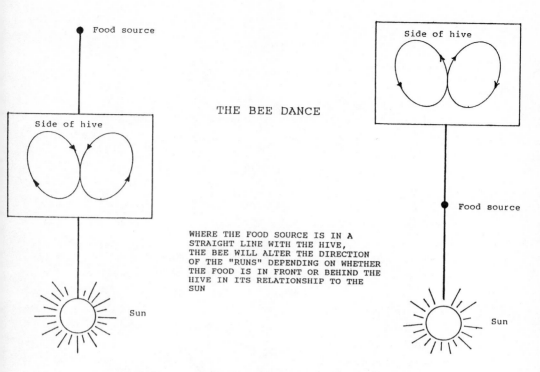

THE BEE DANCE

WHERE THE FOOD SOURCE IS IN A
STRAIGHT LINE WITH THE HIVE,
THE BEE WILL ALTER THE DIRECTION
OF THE "RUNS" DEPENDING ON WHETHER
THE FOOD IS IN FRONT OR BEHIND THE
HIVE IN ITS RELATIONSHIP TO THE
SUN

A "FIGURE OF EIGHT" DANCE WHERE THE FOOD
SOURCE IS MORE THAN 90M AWAY FROM THE HIVE

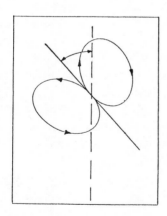
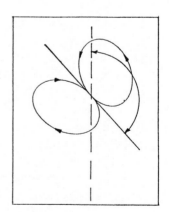

WHERE THE FOOD SOURCE IS AT AN ANGLE
TO THE RIGHT OR LEFT OF A LINE BETWEEN
THE HIVE AND THE POSITION OF THE SUN,
THE BEE WILL UNDERTAKE THE DANCE AT AN
ANGLE COINCIDING WITH THE LOCATION OF
THE FOOD AND ALTER THE DIRECTION OF THE
"RUNS" DEPENDING ON WHETHER THE FOOD IS
TO THE LEFT OR RIGHT OF THE HIVE

Fig. 14 A bee dance

Frogs and Toads

Since much water is wasted by evaporation from the surface of ponds and pools in the garden, especially from waterfalls and fountains, I have not included these items in this book. It is possible, however, to have a small water feature, such as a half-barrel or old enamel sink, sunk to the rim in the garden as a home for aquatic plants and water-loving wildlife such as frogs and toads.

Frogs and toads can be considered the gardener's friends as their diet includes such pests as greenfly, snails, woodlice and slugs. They are prodigious breeders and one female alone can lay up to 2,000 eggs in the spawning season. Despite the production of such high numbers of eggs, there are so many hazards to be faced during the life of the average frog or toad that numbers are drastically reduced. Tadpoles are eaten by fish, birds and other aquatic life and young frogs are the prey of hedgehogs, rats, birds, snakes and domestic cats. They have developed various defence mechanisms, such as skin discoloration and poisonous warts, to discourage predators and despite a drastic reduction in numbers over the past century or so, they may still be seen in most gardens.

Hedgehogs

The hedgehog is a delightful creature and as it can live up to seven or eight years, is of great help to the gardener in reducing the population of slugs, caterpillars and beetles. As it is nocturnal, it is not often seen during the day unless disturbed or hungry, but at night time it becomes a mighty hunter. It makes its home in compost heaps, piles of leaves, under sheds or below hedges, and is one of only three mammals that truly hibernate during the winter, the others being the dormouse and the bat.

Although sometimes attacked by foxes, badgers, dogs, owls, pine martins and pole cats, sadly the worst enemy of the hedgehog is man. In country areas they are disliked and destroyed by gamekeepers because they are wrongly believed to eat the eggs of game birds and are also often killed by vehicles on country roads. In urban areas, however, it is the use of various pesticides that accounts for the premature death of the vast majority. Pesticides placed to kill slugs and other pests are absorbed into the hedgehog's fat reserves and when released, during periods of hibernation, cause great suffering. Such suffering could be avoided if only the gardener realised that the hedgehog is far better at getting rid of pests than the pesticides. In urban areas it would be far better for the gardener to save the money on purchasing slug pellets and attract hedgehogs into the garden instead. Hedgehogs should not be given bread or milk, which are bad for them, but can be given tinned puppy food.

BADGERS

Unlike foxes, which are now quite common both in country and town, the badger is relatively rare. The badger is a country dweller but occasionally may be found around towns and cities. Areas such as Bristol, Bath and Edinburgh have seen an increase in the badger population and, for some reason, the population in Bristol is equal to anything which may be found anywhere in the countryside.

Badgers are mainly nocturnal creatures and rarely appear from their setts until after dark, especially in areas where there is traffic or other human activity. Unlike some other nocturnal creatures, the badger will not spend the whole night hunting but will intersperse periods of activity with short naps, either in its sett or any other dry, safe place.

Although in rural areas the diet of the badger is mainly earthworms, in urban areas it will eat almost anything available, including the contents of any dustbin that can be knocked over. The diet of the urban badger has been known to include cat food, fruit such as apples, plums, pears, blackberries, strawberries and raspberries, and vegetables such as potatoes and carrots. It is not unusual, for instance, for a badger to dig up and clear a complete garden of carrots overnight and if he sets his mind on some tasty fruit, a fruit cage is no barrier.

As badgers are fairly large, strong creatures they may cause considerable damage to a garden, including breaking fences that they feel are in their way. Despite such occasional vandalism, the badger is mainly a peace-loving creature and, apart from man, has very few enemies. Most badgers are killed on the roads, but in urban areas they may be killed by dogs, drowned in swimming pools or become entangled in garden netting. Despite such hazards, a secluded area in a large garden can be one of the safest places for the badger. If you are fortunate enough to have a sett in your garden, the occasional disruption will be far outweighed by the pride and pleasure that these wonderful creatures will give you.

The Grey Squirrel

Grey squirrels are now such a common sight in most gardens that they are often considered a pest. In fact, they were only introduced into this country from America as recently as 1876. Until then, the red squirrel had been native in most parts, but may now only be found in pine forests in some remote areas.

Since the grey is bigger and more adaptable, it quickly took over the feeding grounds of the reds and, to a great extent, has learned to live alongside man. Despite being fun and exciting to watch, with its death-defying leaps from bough to bough high in the canopy of trees, the squirrel causes considerable damage, including digging up bulbs, damaging tree bark, eating herbaceous plants and stealing food put out for birds.

Whilst I appreciate foresters' and horticulturists' dislike of squirrels, I feel that the garden would be a sadder place without them and I do not begrudge my local squirrels the little they steal from my bird table. I can always quickly replace the food and it can be quite fun trying to think up new ways of preventing such theft. So far, the squirrel has always won.

Foxes

The fox is now a common sight both in town and country, although they are comparatively rare in the North of England. Foxes usually live in family groups comprising the dog fox, the vixen and up to five cubs. The group may also include other vixens related to the breeding vixen. Foxes are caring and loving parents and a family with young cubs at play is a delightful sight not soon forgotten.

However, the fox has a very bad reputation for destruction both in the country and town, and in rural areas is thought of as a pest. This may be readily understood if one his witnessed the destruction left behind after a fox has broken into a chicken coop or the cage of a pet rabbit. However, as the fox is not very fussy in its choice of food, in urban areas it feeds mostly on scraps scavenged from dustbins and rubbish heaps.

Moles

I hesitated before including the mole in this list of garden wildlife because it is usually one of the last creatures that the gardener wishes to see in the garden. Despite the fact that the mole is less than 20cm long, it can cause hundreds of pounds' worth of damage to an ornamental lawn in just a few days.

The mole is a solitary creature that spends most of its life underground. It is covered in black, velvety fur and has extremely strong front feet with which it digs tunnels in its search for worms. It is the residue from these tunnelling activities that creates the 'mole hills' which so disfigure the lawn.

Many suggestions have been put forward for getting rid of moles and the mole catcher was once an important part of any rural community. Mole smokes, burning rags, creosote, cats and even the gadget from musical cards have all been used to encourage moles to move on, often with very little effect. If you are unfortunate enough to be visited by a mole, it is best to contact your local council offices who will put you in touch with a mole catcher. This is far better than setting traps or laying bait yourself, as this can cause great pain to the mole and even kill other forms of wildlife.

Helpful Insects in the Garden

I have already mentioned the ladybird as the gardener's friend because of its liking for aphids. There are, however, many other predatory insects, such as hoverflies, lacewings and centipedes, which help reduce the population of harmful insects. In a garden which is free from pesticides and herbicides there may be in excess of 2,000 insect species, the majority of which may be considered the gardener's friend. By finding alternatives to harmful herbicides and pesticides, therefore, the gardener can slowly build up the population of friendly insect predators.

CHAPTER NINE

The Gardener and the General Environment

Who, that has reason, and his smell,
Would not 'mong roses and jasmine dwell,
Rather than all his spirits choke,
With exhalations of dirt and smoke,
And all th'uncleanness which does drown,
In pestilential clouds as pop'lous town.
Abraham Cowley

There has been a very welcome awakening of a 'green' consciousness over the past few years, which stems from a greater common awareness of the need to protect our precious planet. However, many of our future problems as gardeners will be the result of the greenhouse effect, caused by man's lack of care for the general environment over the last 200 years or so.

THE GREENHOUSE EFFECT

Whilst the aim of this chapter is to suggest ways in which the gardener may help the general and local environment, it is worth describing how the greenhouse effect has been caused and how it will affect the way we live in the future.

The greenhouse effect is the result of heat being trapped by the earth's atmosphere. This is caused by an increase in the production of particular gases due to industrial development and the burning of fossil fuels. These gases include carbon dioxide, methane, nitrous oxide and, more recently, CFCs.

The greenhouse effect was first described by Baron Jean Baptiste in 1827 and was linked to industrial pollution by Svante Arrhenius, a Swedish scientist, in 1896. Needless to say, very few people took any notice and our skies and rivers have been constantly raped by pollution since the start of the Industrial Revolution. Although there have been certain restrictions imposed on industry to maintain minimum environmental standards, we only have to look around us to see how ineffective they have been. As man's knowledge of the use of chemicals and gases increased, new pollutants were added to the atmosphere, albeit inadvertently. Moreover, the increasing use of the motor car and a general demand for energy have added considerably to carbon dioxide levels in the atmosphere.

During the 1960s, 1970s and 1980s, governments funded research into the problems caused by pollution, but it was not until the middle of the 1980s that they began to see they had a number of major problems on their hands.

In 1985, Joe Farman and his colleagues at the British Antarctic Survey establishment discovered a hole in the earth's ozone layer, a protective, atmospheric 'skin' surrounding the earth (vital in regulating the whole environment on which life depends) which filters out harmful ultraviolet light. Scientists soon linked this hole to the presence of CFCs in the atmosphere.

Chlorofluorocarbons, known to the world as CFCs, were first developed in the 1930s as a safe cooling agent for refrigerators and air conditioning units. Later, CFCs (invented by Thomas Midgely of General Motors) were also developed as a propellant in spray cans, as the blowing agent for making plastic foam and as a solvent to clean electronic components. CFCs were found not only to damage the ozone layer, but to be among the worst of the greenhouse gases.

The world owes a huge debt of gratitude to Joe Farman and his team as, arguably, it was this catastrophic discovery that brought the whole environmental question to a head and started to bring the world to its senses. Not only was the problem of CFCs and the ozone layer pinpointed, but attention focused on the greenhouse effect and the possible results of global warming. Political parties began to talk 'green' in an effort to win votes and governments began to take international action.

EFFECTS OF GLOBAL WARMING

The most important of the changes caused by the greenhouse effect is the recent increase in the earth's temperature. There have, of course, been many changes in the earth's temperature over millions of years, long before man had any influence over nature. These resulted in wide variations in air and water temperature, from the tropical days during the age of the dinosaurs to the freezing temperatures of the ice ages. It is, however, the incredibly short time in which the recent changes have taken place that is now giving scientists and climatologists great cause for concern.

There has been an increase of 0.5°C in the temperature of the earth since the mid-1800s. This increase is not spread evenly over the earth, but is greater towards the poles. As our tidal and weather systems are based on the distribution of heat around the world, such changes in temperature within individual zones have an immediate effect on the world climate.

Predictions of further increases in the average temperature of the earth's surface due to global warming vary from between 1.5°C to 4.5°C by the middle of the next century unless we drastically reduce the emission of greenhouse gases. As previously mentioned, such a temperature rise would not be evenly distributed. In practice, there could be a huge variation, such as a 0.1°C rise at the tropics and an 8°C rise at the poles.

These zonal changes in the earth's temperature would greatly affect the water levels around our shores due to the melting of the polar caps and an expansion of the seas. Although estimates vary as to the ultimate increase in height of the water level, even the most conservative estimates establish a possible rise in sea level of between 25cm and 30cm by the year 2050. There have even been estimates of an increase of up to 1.65 metres. Such a rise would have a devastating effect on our coastline. In low areas of Great Britain, huge areas of land would be lost to the sea unless coastal defences were improved at immense cost.

In addition to rising water levels, global warming would also influence the air and tidal patterns on a worldwide basis because our tidal and weather systems are based on the distribution of heat around the globe. Such changes would obviously have drastic consequences for all our lives. For gardeners and farmers there may be dramatic shifts in rainfall patterns, and a greater likelihood of droughts for some parts of the country.

Although damage caused by global warming may appear bad enough on its own, it is only one of the many environmental problems that have to be solved if we are to look with hope to the future. The contamination of our rivers and seas; the destruction of the rain forests; the over-use of pesticides and herbicides, all have a major effect on our future.

MAKING OUR OWN MARK ON THE ENVIRONMENT

I have included, later in this chapter, a number of ideas for making our gardening more environmentally acceptable. In themselves, such environmental improvements may seem to have very little effect considering the extent of the problems mentioned previously. However, there is no reason for us to feel inadequate. Although the effect each individual gardener may have is relatively small, as a group, gardeners have immense influence.

For instance, there are somewhere in the region of seventeen million households in this country, of which the majority have gardens. If the owners of these gardens became more environmentally aware and changed their whole lifestyles to suit, the influence on the environment would be enormous.

Here are ten ways in which the gardener can help both the local and worldwide environment.

1)   Think in terms of repair rather than replacement
We live in a throw-away age and it has become usual to discard anything that is slightly damaged or looks old. However, whilst replacement of tools and equipment keeps the suppliers in work, it also uses vast quantities of irreplaceable resources. By replacing this throw-away attitude with one that emphasises maintenance and repair, huge savings in resources could be achieved. Also, if you require any additional garden tools, try to obtain some good second-hand ones. Some of these are of far better quality than the new ones on the market, will last longer and you will be saving those valuable resources.

2)   Forget about gadgets for the garden
Garden centres are full of gadgets, most of which are designed to save the gardener time. Thus there are watering gadgets, weeding gadgets, mowing gadgets, pruning gadgets, hoeing gadgets and hundreds of other gadgets for all the usual gardening tasks. In the majority of cases, these gadgets have been produced at the expense of non-replaceable resources and will

probably be discarded or lost within a few months of purchase. Some may even be made from aluminium, which is formed from mined bauxite and is extremely energy-intensive to produce. Most gardening activities can be undertaken with just a few basic tools and a little hard work. Millions of pounds are spent each year in the keep-fit industry. What better way is there to keep fit than to forget about purchasing garden gadgets to save you time and to expend a little energy in the garden?

3) Start a compost bin
A visit to your local rubbish disposal centre will show you how much garden and household waste is thrown away which could be composted. A recent survey showed that somewhere in the region of four million tonnes of compostable rubbish is produced in this country every year. Such waste, if properly composted, will provide the gardener with bulk material for the garden, rich in nutrients and water retentive properties. By starting and maintaining a healthy compost bin, you will save on the purchase of products such as peat and commercially produced compost; you will also help reduce the cost of rubbish collection and disposal.

4) Try to avoid the use of chemicals
Whilst the major contributory factor to the pollution of the seas is the dumping and discharge of vast quantities of human and industrial waste, an additional factor which is causing concern is the pollution by 'run-off' of water from the land. Run-off is the natural process that occurs when rainwater or melting snow flows overland and discharges into ponds, streams, rivers and lakes, and subsequently into the sea. Run-off is now highly polluted because of the huge increase over the last forty or fifty years in the use of pesticides and fertilisers in agriculture and horticulture. As up to half of the chemicals that are added to the soil may not be taken up by the crop, the remainder is free to gravitate into rivers, lakes and seas. The result may be seen all around us. The lower orders of plant life within rivers and lakes, such as algae, thrive because of the increase in fertilisers. By spreading across the water surface, the algae reduces the oxygen content of the water and other forms of life cannot be sustained. Furthermore, fish absorb high levels of pesticides, which are then taken up in the food chain in animals and birds such as otters and herons.

Until fairly recently, it was quite common practice to use chemicals both in horticulture and agriculture without any thought to the harm caused either to the environment or to the people using them. Lead arsenic and copper arsenic were in common use until the late 1940s and pure nicotine, a few drops of which on the skin can kill, was used during the early part of the century in commercial fruit growing.

Each individual garden is usually relatively small when compared with areas of farmland, and it may seem that the pollution of garden run-off is not of great consequence. However, if one considers the cumulative effect of run-off from all gardens put together, one will immediately recognise that it is imperative that the gardener adapts to life without pesticides and herbicides. Here are a number of ways in which the gardener can help to reduce the use of chemicals.

Avoid the use of disinfectants wherever possible but, where absolutely necessary, employ borax and hot water.

Select wood preservatives that are not injurious to animals, insects and plants.

Avoid any paints that contain methyl chloroform.

Never use or store paraquat, as it is highly toxic.

Plant companion plants, which will reduce the need for artificial pesticides.

Use herbal sprays instead of pesticides and herbicides.

Avoid the use of anything in the garden which will harm hedgehogs as they are one of your best friends in the fight against slugs and other pests.

5)   Provide a wild area
By setting aside an area in your garden in which wildlife will thrive you will be encouraging animals into your garden which will feed on slugs and other garden pests. Within the wild area, leave a pile of sticks and leaves where hedgehogs may safely hibernate. Also, attract hedgehogs into your garden by putting down food and water.

6)   Do not light bonfires
Up until some twenty years ago, one of the pleasures of my life was to light and tend a bonfire in the late autumn. I no longer burn any rubbish from my garden for several reasons.

First, the smoke from a bonfire is indiscriminating in its travels and is most annoying to neighbours. Secondly, much of the material burnt can be composted or recycled in some way. Thirdly, lack of care before lighting a bonfire that has been in position for some time can kill hedgehogs and other hibernating animals. In addition, a large number of items burnt on bonfires have preservatives which give off toxic fumes.

7)   Use only approved hardwoods in the garden
The Friends of the Earth have produced a 'Good Wood Seal of Approval', which indicates items constructed from wood that has not come from rain forests under threat. By selecting products made only from approved woods, you will help reduce the flow of rare wood into this country and, in turn, reduce the incentive to destroy the rain forests.

8)   Consider how the design of your garden will affect the adjacent countryside
When planning your garden, it is extremely important to give consideration to the local environment as this may be greatly affected by your design. For instance, the type of planting you select for your own boundary will greatly influence the atmosphere of the adjacent area. Where the garden boundary is next to farm or park land, formal planting such as a tall hedge of Leyland Cypress will totally spoil the rural aspect of the open land. In such instances, the planting beside the boundary must be of native trees or shrubs and any more formal planting should be confined to areas within the garden.

9)   Think of maintenance requirements when purchasing anything for the garden
Many softwood and metal items used in the garden require constant maintenance if they are always to look their best. Thus a highly formal trellis or summerhouse will need to be painted at least once a year. Such maintenance puts great demands on resources, which could be avoided if alternative materials had been used in the design.

10)   Affect government thought and heighten their awareness
There are a number of ways in which you can help keep environmental issues at the forefront of the government's mind.

Join the C.P.R.E.
In this country there are organisations, such as the Council for the Protection of Rural England, which act not only on behalf of their membership but for all those in Great Britain who care for our countryside. By sub-

scribing or making donations to such organisations we are making a positive effort to preserve what is best in our environment. Other national and worldwide organisations that are concerned with environmental matters include The Countryside Commission; Deep Ecology Workshop/Council for All Beings; Henry Doubleday Research Association; Environmental Research Agency; Friends of the Earth; Greenpeace; The Nature Conservancy Council; Neighbourhood Energy Action; The Ramblers Association; Survival International.

Write to your Member of Parliament
If enough people wrote to their Member of Parliament regarding both local and global environmental issues, the government would be under immense pressure to take environmental issues seriously.

CHAPTER TEN

What of the Future?

Go little book, and wish to all
Flowers in the garden, meat in the hall,
A bin of wine, a spice of wit,
A house with lawns enclosing it,
A living river by the door,
A nightingale in the sycamore.
Robert Louis Stevenson, *Underwoods*

When one considers the environmental disasters of the last 200 years, it is very clear that, even if major improvements are made immediately in the way we treat the environment, how we garden in the future will greatly depend on the climatic changes that have already taken place worldwide. Unless we protect our gardens with an environmentally controlled glass dome, the changes in temperature, air and tide patterns and the effect of pollution that have taken place must affect the ways we approach our gardening and will continue to do so for many years to come.

We are already able to see the effects of these environmental changes on a worldwide scale – our television screens are constantly showing examples of water and air pollution, acid rain and soil erosion. Areas of once fertile land are being turned into desert and crops are being devastated by plagues of insects which are multiplying because of climatic changes.

The realisation of the effect such changes in the climate would have on the lives of gardeners and horticulturalists in Great Britain came to me on a very hot, dry day in June 1989 whilst I was surveying a garden at Angmering on Sea with a colleague. It was not the high temperature, the dryness of the ground or the fact that there was already a very strict ban on the use of water which brought about this awareness, but the number of greenfly in the garden. I had already heard warnings that there was to be a plague of aphids and other unwelcome insects because of the high temperature and dry conditions, but nothing had prepared me for the experience of intimate contact with so many of these horrible little creatures. The garden was packed with fully developed shrubs and trees, through which we had to force a way in order to take our measurements. Within a few minutes we were both covered in fat, healthy greenfly that seemed to get everywhere. By the end of the day I felt as if I had not washed for weeks and I can still remember the pleasure of showering away the filth as soon as I arrived home.

This memory, unimportant as it may be, is just one example of how our gardens may be affected by changes in our environment and how we are forced to adapt to accommodate them.

The two years 1989 and 1990 were both very dry and temperatures were extremely high. Throughout 1991, rainfall was generally below average for much of south and eastern England, with record reductions in groundwater reserves. The winter of 1991/92 again saw well below average rainfall in many parts of the country as the fourth year of continuous drought began. Real problems of restricted water supply, dried-up rivers and crop failures became apparent during 1992.

It must be recognised that problems of water shortage are no longer a local matter. There has got to be a reappraisal, from the European Community level downwards, of the way we use water. The general public must constantly be reminded of the need to save water.

Practical ways forward may include the recycling of water for industrial use; the use of new technology to reduce the need for water from rivers and the sea: reduction in the water loss through leakage from supply systems; the transfer of water via a national water grid; the introduction of water metering into all industrial, commercial and private premises, and the introduction of an environmental audit to establish the monetary savings related to the better use of water reserves.

Further variations in the climate will demand constant revisions in our approach to water use and other environmental issues and, although it is impossible to foretell what the future will bring, it is obvious that we must all approach the problems in a positive way and adapt to whatever climatic conditions are presented. It is clear that we must all learn to work together to ensure a better world for future generations.

In this context I am reminded of a film I saw in 1989. The film showed the incredible force of Hurricane Gilbert as it swept its way across the Caribbean and Mexico in 1988. It concentrated on how the people in the path of the hurricane coped, both in preparation and in re-establishing their lives afterwards. One saw, with the clarity that good television can provide, how these people prepared their town and individual properties. Cattle were all herded to places of safety; everything loose was battened down; windows and doors were boarded up, and tarpaulins were tied over roofs to prevent the loss of tiles. The film showed the development of the storm and there were some dramatic pictures of cars being overturned and barn doors flying through the air like pieces of paper. When the storm passed, the whole township emerged to survey the effects of the hurricane. Despite sustaining considerable damage, the general consensus of opinion was that, because everyone had heeded the warnings and all reacted together, they had got away lightly.

Let us hope and pray that when the present 'environmental' storm has passed, we will be able to say the same thing and look with certainty to the future.

List of Trees and Plants Resistant to Drought

In order to grow healthily and reproduce, plants require water, oxygen, nutrients, sunlight and anchorage in the soil. The structure of plants has developed, over millions of years, so that they are now highly efficient at extracting energy from the sun and soil. Each of the main parts of a plant – the roots, stem and leaves – serves a specific purpose.

The Root System

Root systems provide anchorage and the fine root hairs take up water and nutrients from the soil. It is imperative that the root system develops well if all other parts of the plant are to function properly.

The Stem

The stem holds the plant up to the sunlight, presents the flowers to encourage fertilisation and holds up fruit seeds for dispersal. The structure of the stem depends greatly on the length of the plant's life: comparatively long-living plants, such as shrubs and trees, have strong, woody stems; annuals, which are short-lived, have soft, sappy stems.

The Leaves

The leaves contain chlorophyll for photosynthesis, which is the process by which green plants manufacture sugars and starch from sunlight. They also control the temperature of the plant by transpiration, which is the evaporation of moisture from the leaf surface. Also, in some climbers, the leaves are adapted to support the plant by throwing off tendrils.

Selecting trees and plants for drought conditions is always difficult and often unsatisfactory. For example, the plant that is able to survive for long periods without water in a dry summer may suffer badly from having its roots waterlogged during a subsequent wet winter. Selection has been made even more difficult recently by the high winds in some parts of the country in late summer and autumn.

The trees and plants included in this list are those that generally show some resistance to varying periods without water, once fully established. However, where good, water-retentive organic material is added to the soil, many other plants may be added to this list.

Although a genus of the plants listed may consist of several hundred species, varieties and cultivars, only a small percentage may be suitable for drought conditions. Therefore, care must be taken when selecting different species, varieties or cultivars.

The common plant names are indicated in brackets where applicable. Many plants have more than one common name (that is the problem with the common naming of plants), and I have chosen the one that I feel is most used.

Plant Name	Description	Uses	Restrictions	Species/Varieties
Abelia × grandiflora	semi-evergreen, pink-flowering shrub	wall shrub on south-facing wall	only hardy in very mild regions	
Abutilon vitifolium	large, upright, deciduous shrub	wall shrub on south-facing wall	not hardy, requires protection	A. vitifolium: 'Tennant's White', 'Veronica Tennant'
Acanthus spinosus (Bear's Breeches)	tall, hardy, herbaceous perennial	to provide height and colour to the mixed border	requires well-drained soil in sun or light shade	
Acer (Maple)	large genus of deciduous trees	good autumn colour, some with interesting bark colour and texture	requires protection from frosts and wind when young	A. campestre (Field Maple) A. ginnala A. negundo (Box Elder): 'Aureum', 'Californicum', 'Elegans' 'Flamingo', 'Variegatum' A. platanoides (Norway Maple): 'Columnare', 'Crimson King', 'Drummondii', 'Erectum', 'Globosum' 'Laciniatum', 'Royal Red', 'Schwedleri' A. pseudoplatanus (Sycamore): 'Atropurpureum', 'Brilliantissimum' 'Corstorphinense', 'Leopoldii', 'Luteovirens', 'Simon Louis Freres', 'Worleei' A. saccharinum (Sugar Maple):

Plant Name	Description	Uses	Restrictions	Species/Varieties
Achillea (Yarrow)	hardy, herbaceous perennial	fern-like leaves brighten borders and add textural interest	tall varieties require cutting back in early winter. Needs well-drained soil in full sun	A. chrysocoma A. clavennae A. clypeolata A. coronation gold A. eupatorium A. filipendulina A. lewisii A. millefolium A. ptarmica A. taygetea A. tomentosa A. × Kelleri A. × King Edward
Aesculus (Horse Chestnut)	deciduous, hardy, flowering tree	large focal point with good colour	can grow to height of 10 m	A. × Carnea (Red Horse Chestnut) A. flava (Sweet Buckeye) A. hippocastanum (Common Horse Chestnut) A. indica (Indian Horse Chestnut) A. parvia (Red Buckeye): 'Humilis' A parviflora
Aethionema × Warley Rose	deep pink-flowering, hardy perennial	as ground cover or in rock gardens	requires full sun and well-drained soil	
Agave americana	cactus-like, greenhouse perennial	focal point for formal bedding	not at all hardy. Dies after flowering at maturity, which may be fifty years old or more	A. americana: 'Marginata', 'Mediopicta'
Ailanthus altissima (Tree of Heaven)	attractive, flowering, deciduous tree	small specimen tree grown for its interesting foliage	hardy only to −10°C	A. altissima: 'Erythrocarpa', 'Pendulifolia'
Amelanchier lamarckii (June Berry)	small, spring-flowering, deciduous tree	fine specimen tree with good autumn foliage colour	requires good, rich soil	

Name	Description	Use	Notes	Varieties
Anchusa azurea	blue-flowering, herbaceous perennial	best mass-planted in mixed borders	requires support and may be damaged by wind	A. azurea: 'Dropmore', 'Loddon Royalist', 'Morning Glory', 'Royal Blue'
Antirrhinum majus (Snapdragon)	multicoloured, hardy perennial	bedding plant for large borders	support required for tall varieties	A. majus: 'Bright Butterfly', 'Cheerio Mixture', Cinderella Mixed', 'Hummingbird', 'Sweetheart'
Arbutus × andrachnoides (Strawberry Tree)	small, deciduous tree	specimen tree of particular interest for red, peeling bark	only hardy in milder regions	
Artemisia 'Powys Castle'	deciduous or semi-evergreen shrub	best grown against south-facing wall	should not be considered hardy	
Alyssum saxatile (Madwort)	low, golden-yellow flowering perennial	rock gardens and dry stone walls	vulnerable to slug damage	A. saxatile: 'Compactum', 'Citrinum', 'Plenum', 'Variegatum'
Aralia elata (Angelica Tree)	small, white-flowering, deciduous tree	as specimen tree or strong focal point	leaves may be scorched by strong winds	A. elata: 'Aureovariegata', 'Variegata'
Armeria juniperina (Thrift)	hardy, pink-flowering, evergreen perennial	rock gardens or as edging plant in mixed borders	may be affected by rust	A. juniperina 'Bevan's Variety'
Aubrieta deltoidea	low-growing, hardy, evergreen perennial	dry walls, rock gardens	requires well-drained, alkaline soil in full sun	A. deltoidea: 'Aurea', 'Barker's Double', 'Godstone', 'Riverslea'
Ballota pseudodictamnus	small, pink-flowering, evergreen shrub	fine foliage; one of the best plants for underplanting roses	not considered hardy	
Begonia semperflorens	dwarf, fibrous-rooted, bedding plant	for bedding out in full sun	not hardy, best grown as houseplant	B. semperflorens: 'Danica Scarlet', 'Flamingo', 'Indian Maid', 'Organdy'
Berberis (Barberry)	interesting, hardy, deciduous shrub	attractive for form, flowering and berries	care should be taken when selecting and placing Berberis as some have vicious thorns	B. aggregata B. wilsoniae B. stenophylla

Plant Name	Description	Uses	Restrictions	Species/Varieties
Betula pendula (Silver Birch)	small to medium, hardy, deciduous tree	grown singly or in groups; often grown for its interesting and attractive bark	generally short-lived	*B. pendula*: 'Dalecarlica' 'Fastigiata', 'Purpurea', 'Tristis' 'Youngii'
Buddleia davidii (Butterfly Bush)	large, hardy, deciduous, flowering shrub	attractive to butterflies	requires cutting back in early spring or it will become straggly and flowering will be reduced	*B. davidii*: 'Black Knight', 'Border Beauty', 'Darkness', 'Empire Blue', 'Fascination' 'Harlequin', 'Ile de France', 'Nanho Alba', 'Nanho Blue', 'Opera' 'Orchid Beauty', 'Royal Red', 'White Bouquet', 'White Cloud', 'White Profusion'
Buxus sempervirens (Common Box)	hardy, evergreen shrub	good, all-round shrub for hedging, topiary and structural planting	may be extremely slow-growing	*B. sempervirens*: 'Aurea Maculata Pendula', 'Elegantissima', 'Gold Tip', 'Handsworthensis', 'Latifolia Maculata', 'Pyramidalis' 'Rotundifolia', 'Suffruticosa'
Calamintha nepetoides	bushy, blue-flowering, hardy perennial	lush, green, aromatic foliage adds colour and texture to borders	requires chalk soil in full sun	
Calandrinia umbellata (Rock Purslane)	bright, crimson-flowering perennial	rock gardens, dry areas or edging	not hardy, best treated as an annual	
Callistemon linearis (Bottle Brush)	pink-flowering, evergreen shrub	best grown as wall shrub for its flowers	not considered hardy, requires acid soil	
Caragana arborescens (Pea Tree)	hardy, yellow-flowering, deciduous tree	attractive foliage, good autumn colour	best in full sun or light shade	*C. arborescens*: 'Lorbergii', 'Pendula', 'Walker'
Carex (Sedge)	evergreen, grass-like, hardy perennial	for textural interest in mixed borders in full sun	requires good, rich soil	*C. buchananii* *C. comans* *C. flagellifera* *C. gravi*

Plant	Type	Use	Notes	Cultivars
Carpinus betulus (Common Hornbeam)	hardy, small to medium, deciduous tree	good for hedging, also attractive specimen tree when matured	young plants must not be allowed to dry out	*C. betulus*: 'Fastigiata', 'Incisa', 'Purpurea', 'Pyramidalis'
Caryopteris × clandonensis	hardy, flowering, deciduous shrub	for its aromatic, grey-green foliage	needs protection in cold regions	*C. × clandonensis*: 'Arthur Simmonds', 'Ferndown', 'Heavenly Blue', 'Kew Blue'
Catananche caerulea (Cupid's Dart)	blue-flowering, hardy, herbaceous perennial	good for cutting and drying	fairly short-lived	*C. caerulea*: 'Bicolour', 'Major', 'Perry's White'
Ceanothus thyrsiflorus 'Blue Mound'	blue-flowering, hardy, evergreen shrub	for structural planting where protected from cold winds and frost	best against a south-facing wall	*C. thyrsiflorus* 'Repens'
Cedrus atlantica	large, evergreen tree	as large and well-shaped focal point	requires rich soil; stake young trees to encourage development of correct shape	*C. atlantica*: 'Glauca', 'Fastigiata', 'Pendula'
Celosia argentia	summer bedding annuals	in mixed border for foliage and flower	requires rich but well-drained soil in a sunny, protected position	
Centaurea dealbata 'John Coutts'	pink-flowering, herbaceous perennial	for the effect of its silver-grey foliage in mixed borders	requires full sun and good drainage	
Ceratostigma willmottianum	half-hardy, blue-flowering, deciduous shrub	mixed borders in mild regions	requires some protection when young	
Cercidiphyllum japonicum (Katsura Tree)	medium-sized, hardy, deciduous, tree	fine specimen tree with good autumn colour	young foliage may be damaged by frost	*C. japonicum* 'Pendulum'
Cercis siliquastrum (Judas Tree)	medium, deciduous, flowering tree	as fine specimen tree in full sun	flowers may be damaged by late frost; requires shelter in cold regions	

Plant Name	Description	Uses	Restrictions	Species/Varieties
Cheiranthus cheiri (Wallflower)	species of wallflower grown as biennials	in mixed border; provides interesting flower colour and scent	requires good drainage and alkaline soil	C. cheiri: 'Blood Red', Carmine King', 'Fire King', 'Eastern Queen', 'Ivory White', 'Tom Thumb'
Chionodoxa luciliae (Glory of the Snow)	bulb with light blue and white flowers	for the front of mixed border in full sun	needs good drainage; attractive to slugs	C. luciliae: 'Alba', 'Rosea'
Chrysanthemum parthenium	free-flowering, hardy annual	for edging or in mixed border	requires well-drained, poor soil	C. parthenium 'Aureum'
Cistus (Rock Rose)	flowering, evergreen shrub	intermediate ground cover in full sun	not hardy in cold regions; likes poor soil	C.: 'Silver Pink', 'Sunset' C. laurifolius C. × corbariensis C. loretii
Clarkia elegans	summer-flowering, hardy annual	adds height to the front of mixed border	best in full sun with slightly acid soil	C. elegans 'Firebrand'
Clerodendrum trichotomum	large, flowering, deciduous shrub	for flower and fruit interest in protected areas	requires sun, shelter and good drainage	C. trichotomum 'Fargesii'
Colutea arborescens (Bladda Senna)	large, hardy, deciduous shrub	often grown for its colourful fruit pods	requires full sun	C. arborescens 'Copper Beauty'
Convolvulus cneorum	half-hardy, white-flowering, evergreen shrub	neat shrub for mixed borders	requires sunny, sheltered location	C. tricolor 'Blue Flash'
Cordyline australis (Cabbage Palm)	attractive, tender, evergreen shrub	as architectural plant or focal point against a wall	only considered hardy in mild regions	C. australis 'Purpurea'
Coreopsis drummondii	attractive, yellow-flowering annual	to highlight a yellow or purple border in full sun	requires support in an open, sunny site	C. drummondii 'Golden Crown'
Corokia cotoneaster (Wire Netting Bush)	small, intertwining evergreen shrub with	as special interest plant for its unusual shape and habit	requires full sun	

Name	Description	Use	Requirements	Species/Cultivars
Coromilla emeris	evergreen, yellow-flowering shrub	to highlight the border in March and April	requires a warm, sheltered position	*C. glauca*
Cortaderia (Pampas Grass)	tall, evergreen, perennial grass	to add height and texture	becomes straggly; best in sunny, sheltered position; requires well-drained soil	*C. argentia*, *C. richardii*, *C. selloana*
Corydalis lutea	yellow-flowering, low-growing, hardy perennial with fern-like leaves	for textural interest in dry locations	requires full sun and well-drained soil	
Corylus avellana	medium, nut-bearing, deciduous tree	as large focal point; spring interest provided by yellow catkins	requires well-drained soil in full sun or partial shade and protection from east winds	*C. avellana*: 'Aurea', 'Contorta'
Cosmos sulphureus	free-flowering, half-hardy annual	as long-lived, yellow-flowered plant to highlight area of mixed border	requires poor soil in sun; provide support	*C. sulphureus*: 'Gloria', 'Klondyke' 'Psyche', 'Sunset'
Cotinus coggygria (Smoke Tree)	large, hardy, deciduous shrub	for brilliant autumn colour and texture	requires well-drained soil in full sun	*C. coggygria*: 'Atropurpureus', 'Foliis Purpureis', 'Royal Purple'
Cotoneaster conspicuus	large, hardy, arching, evergreen shrub	as structural plant; for colour of white flowers in June and red berries in autumn	best in full sun	*C. conspicuus* 'Decorous'
Crambe cordifolia	large, white-flowering, hardy perennial	as specimen plant in mixed border for its foliage	requires well-drained, alkaline soil sheltered from winds	
Crataegus monogyna (Common Hawthorn)	medium, flowering, hardy, deciduous tree	good for a large, compact hedge or screen	requires open, sunny position	*C. monogyna*: 'Biflora', 'Stricta'
Crepis rubra	compact, white- or red-flowering annual	adds bright colour to mixed border in August	requires well-drained soil in full sun	

Plant Name	Description	Uses	Restrictions	Species/Varieties
Crocus	popular, hardy, small, flowering bulb	for bright colour in mixed border in spring	requires well-drained soil in a protected area	C. *aureus* C. *balansae* C. *corsicus* C. *biflorus* C. *dalmaticus* C. *etruscus* C. *goulimyi* C. *longiflorus* C. *minimus* C. *nudiflorus* C. *sativus* C. *vernus*
Cupressus glabra (Cypress)	interesting evergreen conifer, reaching height of 15–20m	as specimen tree for its blue-green foliage	requires well-drained soil in full sun with some protection from cold winds	C. *glabra*: 'Conica', 'Pyramidalis'
Cynoglossum nervosum (Hounds Tongue)	blue-flowering, herbaceous perennial	in mixed border for foliage and colour interest	requires support and rich but well-drained soil in sun or light shade	
Cytisus (Broom)	hardy, flowering, deciduous shrub	as intermediate plant for neutral to acid soils; hardy to −10°C	requires full sun	C.: 'Cornish Cream', 'Daisy Hill', 'Dragonfly', 'Fulgens', 'Golden Sunlight', 'Goldfinch', 'Hollandia' 'Killiney Red', 'Queen Mary', 'Redwings', 'Windlesham Ruby', 'Zeelandia' C. × *beanii* C. × *kewensis* C. × *praecox*: 'Albus', 'Allgold'
Daphne mezereum	small, winter-flowering, deciduous, hardy shrub	for winter interest as intermediate planting in mixed border	hardy only to 10 C; requires well-drained soil	D. *mezereum*: 'Alba', 'Alba Bowle's Hybrid', 'Grandiflora', 'Rubrum'
Delphinium ajacis	tall, blue- or violet-	adds colour and height to mixed border	requires, sunny, protected site	

Name	Description	Use	Requirements	Species/Varieties
Deutzia × hybrida	early summer-flowering, deciduous, hardy shrub	adds colour to sunny borders	needs protection from cold winds; young growth may be damaged by late frosts	*D. × hybrida*: 'Contraste', 'Magician', 'Mont Rose', 'Perle Rose'
Dianthus (Pinks and Carnations)	large genus of annuals and evergreen perennials	adds bright colour to beds, borders and rock gardens; good for cutting and button holes	requires well-drained soil in full sun	*D. alpinus* *D. barbatus* *D. chinensis* *D. deltoides*
Dimorphotheca barberiae	bright purple-pink flowering perennial	adds colour, scent and texture to the front of mixed border	requires well-drained soil in protected but sunny position; should be considered tender in most parts of the country	*D. barberiae* 'Compacta'
Dorycnium hirsutum	low spreading, flowering, deciduous shrub	for late summer and autumn interest; especially useful for the white or grey border	requires well-drained soil in full sun	
Draba aizoides	low-growing, hardy perennial with masses of rich, yellow flowers in April	adds colour to front of a yellow border where local watering is not a problem	requires moist soil during growing and early flowering periods only	
Echium lycopsis	blue- or purple-flowering, hardy annual	adds colour and texture to mixed border	requires open, sunny site	*E. lycopsis* 'Blue Bedder'
Elaeagnus × ebbingei	large, quick-growing evergreen shrub	for structural planting, hedges, screens and coastal planting	best in sun or partial shade	*E. angustifolia* *E. commutata* *E. pungens*
Elsholtzia stauntonii	unusual, autumn-flowering shrub	intermediate planting in shrub or mixed border, giving flower and foliage interest	requires full sun; only hardy to −5°C	
Eremurus (Foxtail Lilly)	hardy, herbaceous perennial with striking spikes of star-shaped flowers in late spring	for both flower and form in mixed border	requires sunny position but must be protected from early morning sunlight	*E. elwesii* *E. himalaicus* *E. robusta*

Plant Name	Description	Uses	Restrictions	Species/Varieties
Eryngium tripartitum	blue-flowering, herbaceous perennial	adds texture to mixed border	requires sunny position	
Eschscholzia californica	poppy-like, hardy annual with bright orange-yellow, summer flowers	adds both colour and texture to mixed border	requires poor, well-drained soil in full sun	*E. californica*: 'Ballerina', 'Cherry Ripe', 'Mission Bells', 'Monarch Art Shades'
Eucalyptus (Gum Tree)	interesting genus of trees and shrubs that have become very popular for their young foliage	often grown for its interesting bark and young foliage; some varieties form a large tree	requires well-drained soil in full sun; young plants need watering in drought conditions	*E. gunnii* *E. niphophila*
Euodia hupehensis	extremely slow-growing, late summer-flowering, medium-height, evergreen tree	adds white flower colour to the garden in late summer and early autumn	for dry conditions and is best in acid soils	
Euonymus japonica (Spindle Tree)	large, evergreen shrub	as structural plant variegated forms often grown for bold foliage	variegated forms only hardy to −5°C and will not variegate properly in deep shade	*E. japonica*: 'Albomarginatus', 'Aureopictus', 'Macrophyllus', 'Macrophyllus Albus', 'Macrophyllus Aureus', 'Ovatus Aureus'
Euryops acraeus	small, silver-grey leaved, evergreen shrub with yellow flowers in late spring	adds bright yellow to protected bed or border	may require some protection from frost and winds in cold regions of the country	
Fagus sylvatica (Common Beech)	large, hardy, deciduous tree with fine bronze-yellow autumn foliage	as large focal point when grown singly; as windbreak; also forms a fine avenue	slow-growing when first planted	*F. sylvatica*: 'Albovariegata', 'Cockleshell', 'Fastigiata', 'Purpurea'
Foeniculum vulgare (Fennel)	tall, aromatic, culinary herb	adds texture and form to mixed border; for culinary purposes	requires well-drained soil in full sun	*F. vulgare*: 'Giant Bronze', 'Purpureum'

Name	Description	Use	Conditions	Species/varieties
Forsythia suspensa	large, rich, yellow-flowering, deciduous shrub with drooping branches	adds a mass of colour to beds and borders in March and April; also acts as good wall shrub for any aspect	can appear untidy if planted in a formal arrangement	
Fraxinus ornus (Manna Ash)	hardy, medium, deciduous tree with off-white, attractive flowers in late spring	large focal point; as it is extremely hardy, it forms a good windbreak	best in full sun	
Fremontodendron californica	golden-yellow flowering deciduous shrub	for foliage and flower interest; may be trained against a trellis	requires well-drained soil and full sun	*F. californica:* 'California Glory', 'California Gold'
Gaillardia aristata (Blanket Flower)	colourful perennial with large, dramatic, daisy-like flowers and soft, grey-green foliage	to highlight an area of border; good for cut flowers	requires well-drained soil in full sun	
Gazania	small, tender, herbaceous perennial with daisy-like flowers	for containers, cutting and bedding out when all threats of frost have gone	usually grown as annuals because of vulnerability to frost; requires well-drained soil in full sun	*G. rigens* *G.* × *hybrida*
Genista hispanica (Broom)	small, hardy, bright, yellow-flowering, deciduous shrub forming a low mound	as intermediate planting for a large border with strong summer flower interest	best in well-drained, neutral or acid soil	*G. aetnensis* *G. lydia* *G. pilosa* *G. tinctoria:* 'Plena', 'Royal Gold'
Geranium	large genus of hardy, herbaceous perennials with attractive flowers and foliage	no mixed border would be complete without a selection or hardy geraniums; however, colours should be selected with care	support required for tall varieties	*G. cinereum* *G. endressii* 'Wargrave Pink' *G. grandiflorum* *G. macrorrhizum* 'Ingwersen's Variety' *G. psilostemon* 'Johnson's Blue'

Plant Name	Description	Uses	Restrictions	Species/Varieties
Gladiolus byzantinus (Sword Lily)	large genus of extremely showy, half-hardy bulbous plants	as startling addition to mixed border or for cut flowers	will dominate all adjacent plants in the border if not selected and planted with care; requires well-drained soil in full sun	G. callianthus G. tristus
Gleditsia triacanthos	large range of deciduous trees with attractive foliage	as small to large focal point; also provides deep shade	only hardy down to −10°C; requires a rich but well-drained soil	G. triacanthos: 'Bujoti', 'Ruby Lace', 'Sunburst'
Gypsophila repens	low growing, mat-forming alpine	rock gardens or dry walls	requires well-drained soil in full sun	G. repens: 'Fratensis', 'Rosea' (syn. G. prostrata rosea)
Halimium ocymoides	low growing, bright yellow and black-flowering, deciduous shrub	colourful shrub for the front of the border or for rock gardens	requires full sun and protection from cold winds	
Hebe	evergreen, flowering shrubs	decorative flower and interesting foliage for mixed border	some are tender and require protection	H. albicans H. 'Armstrongii' H. 'Autumn Glory' H. buchananii H. cupressoides H. macrantha H. pinguifolia 'Pagei'
Hedysarum multijugum	medium to large, purple-flowering, deciduous shrub	adds colour to mixed border	requires sunny position	
Helianthemum nummularium	low growing, spreading, evergreen shrub	rock gardens	may be invasive to other, less vigorous plants; requires full sun	H. nummularium: 'Ben Nevis', 'Fireball', 'Jubilee', 'Mrs Earle'
Helianthus annuus (Sunflower)	extremely tall, large yellow-flowering, hardy annual	good plant for children to grow	does not integrate in a border; requires well-drained soil in full sun	H. annuus: 'Autumn Beauty', 'Flore Pleno', 'Russian Giant'

Plant	Description	Use	Conditions	Varieties
Helichrysum rosmarinifolius (Snow in Summer)	large, narrow, erect, evergreen shrub with profusion of white flowers in midsummer	excellent for adding height to large border and good for children to grow	requires well-drained soil in full sun	
Hibiscus syriacus	large, upright but branching deciduous shrub with large flowers July–October	fine addition to large border	although it is hardy down to −15°C, flower buds may be damaged by late frost; requires well-drained soil	*H. syriacus*: 'Admiral Dewey', 'Ardens', 'Blue Bird', 'Elegantissimus', 'Hamabo', 'Lady Stanley', 'Leopoldi', 'Pink Giant', 'Russian Violet', 'W.R. Smith'
Hippophae rhamnoides	large, hardy, deciduous shrub	grown mainly for its bright orange autumn berries	only female plants have berries and require planting next to a male; needs full sun or partial shade	
Iberis amara (Candytuft)	impressive, hardy annual with aromatic leaves	adds colour and texture to border	requires full sun	
Ilex aquifolium (Holly)	evergreen shrub or tree planted for its foliage and attractive berries	as structural plant once fully grown; variegated forms give all-year-round interest; often used as Christmas decorations	very slow-growing; variegated forms require sunny position	*I. aquifolium*: 'Angustifolia', 'Argenteo-marginata Pendula', 'Aurea-marginata', 'Golden Queen', 'Handsworth New Silver', 'Pyramidalis', 'Silver Milkboy'
Indigofera potaninii	large, rose-pink-flowering, deciduous shrub	adds colour to large border in early summer	requires well-drained soil in full sun	
Iris tectorum	hardy, crested Iris which reaches a height of 45cm, with large attractive flowers in early summer	adds colour to border	requires semi-shaded and protected site	*I. tectorum*: 'Alba', 'Variegata'
Jasminum nudiflorum (Jasmin)	large, untidy, yellow-flowering, deciduous shrub which is hardy in most parts of Britain	showy, winter-flowering plant for very large, informal border	flowers may be scorched by cold winds	

Plant Name	Description	Uses	Restrictions	Species/Varieties
Juniperus chinensis (Juniper)	attractive, tall, narrow conifer	strong focal point	some forms may lose their shape when fully mature	*J. chinensis*: 'Aurea', 'Kuriwao Gold'
Kniphofia (Red Hot Poker)	hardy, herbaceous perennials with striking flowers; some have extremely 'hot' colours	to highlight areas of mixed border	will not thrive in rich soil; requires full sun	
Kochia scorparia	impressive, half-hardy annual with attractive autumn foliage colour	adds foliage colour to autumn border	best in an open, sunny border	
Koelreuteria paniculata	small, hardy, deciduous tree with interesting foliage and bark	as specimen tree in medium to large garden	requires full sun and does not like alkaline soil	*K. paniculata* 'Fastigiata'
Kolkwitzia amabilis	tall, upright, hardy, deciduous shrub with arching branches and pink flowers in summer	in a large border for a show of flowers in summer	requires well-drained soil in full sun	*K. amabilis* 'Pink Cloud'
Laburnum (Golden Rain Tree)	well-known, yellow-flowering, deciduous shrub or small tree	grown mostly for its impressive yellow flowers	as this plant is poisonous, it must not be grown where children or animals may eat the seeds	*L. alpinum* 'Pendulum' *L.* × *watereri* 'Vossii'
Lagurus ovatus	hardy annual grass approx. 30cm tall	excellent addition to mixed border for form and texture; may be pot grown; leaves can be used in flower arranging	requires well-drained soil in full sun	
Laurus nobilis (Sweet Bay)	large, hardy, evergreen shrub	for structural planting in large border; may be pot grown; leaves can be used in cooking	leaves may be scorched by cold winds; requires sunny but sheltered position	*L. nobilis*: 'Angustifolia', 'Aurea'

Name	Description	Uses	Requirements	Cultivars
Lavandula angustifolia (Lavender)	small, evergreen shrub	for edging borders and as low-growing hedge	protect from cold winds	*L. angustifolia*: 'Alba', 'Folgate', 'Hidcote', 'Munstead', 'Rosea'
Lavatera olbia (Mallow)	large, pink-flowering, deciduous shrub	attractive summer flower colour and upright habit	grows poorly in anything but full sun; requires protection as it is only hardy down to −5°C; requires hard pruning in spring	
Layia elegans	atttractive, yellow-flowering, hardy annual that grows to height of 45cm	for its pleasant grey-green foliage and daisy-like flower in sunny border	does best in well-drained soil	
Leptosiphon hybridus	low-growing annual with tiny but very attractive flowers in summer	excellent for rock gardens, window boxes and other containers; also good for cracks in paving	requires sunny, open position in well-drained soil	*L. hybridus*: 'French Hybrids', 'Rainbow Mixture'
Lespedeza thunbergii	rose-purple flowering, deciduous shrub	for intermediate planting in large mixed border and to provide autumn colour	requires rich but well-drained soil in full sun	*L. thunbergii* 'Alba Flora'
Leycesteria formosa	very interesting deciduous shrub providing fruit and flower colour	excellent for integrated or massed planting in mixed border	does not grow well in very alkaline soils; only hardy down to −10°C; fruits are very attractive to insects	
Ligustrum ovalifolium (Privet)	hardy, semi-evergreen shrub	often used for hedging and screening; variegated forms are excellent background for some of the purple-leafed *Berberis*	does not grow well in poor alkaline soil; may lose its leaves in cold regions	*L. ovalifolium*: 'Argenteum', 'Aureum'
Limnanthus douglasii (Poached Egg Flower)	low-growing, hardy annual with white and yellow flowers; attractive to bees	as edging plant or in rock gardens	requires an open site; will grow best when mulched	

Plant Name	Description	Uses	Restrictions	Species/Varieties
Linaria maroccana (Toadflax)	narrow, upright annual with boldly coloured flowers	grown in groups, they provide a mass of colour to borders in summer; also very good for container planting	requires well-drained soil in full sun	L. maroccana 'Fairy Bouquet'
Lippia citriodora	aromatic, deciduous, flowering shrub	as small, open, branching shrub, best grown against a south-facing wall	should not be considered hardy in any but the mildest regions of Britain	
Lobularia maritima (Sweet Alyssum)	low-growing annual covered in clusters of small white or mauve flowers from June to September	excellent for rock gardens, dry walls and cracks in paving	best in full sun	L. maritima: 'Carpet of Snow', 'Little Dorrit', 'Oriental Night', 'Rosie O'Day', 'Royal Carpet', 'Snow Drift', 'Wonderland'
Lonicera nitida	medium-sized, evergreen shrub	for intermediate planting; forms a good low hedge; interesting shrub to plant with others that have leaves of different sizes or textures	becomes straggly if not trimmed; good soil preparation is a must	L. nitida 'Baggessen's Gold'
Lunaria annua (Honesty)	purple-flowered biennial which grows to height of 75cm	adds summer colour and textural interest to border	requires slightly shaded position in well-prepared soil	L. annua: 'Alba', 'Variegata'
Mentzelia lindleyi	medium to tall, hardy annual with large, golden-yellow flowers in summer	for flower and foliage interest in border	best in light, fertile soil in a sunny position	
Mesembryanthemum criniflorum	dazzling, low-growing annuals with daisy-like flowers in summer	with some care they can be included in the rock garden, but are not plants that will integrate well	must have full sun in well-drained soil	
Muscari armeniacum (Grape Hyacinth)	delightful, bulbous plant with blue and white flowers in late spring	best mass-planted at the front of the border; also excellent for rock gardens	grows best in well-drained soil but must have a sunny site	M. armeniacum 'Heavenly Blue'

Name	Description	Use	Conditions	Varieties
Nepeta × faassenii (Catmint)	herbaceous perennial with spikes of lavender blue flowers in summer	for massed planting at the edge of a mixed border	*Nepeta* is attractive to cats, which like to roll in it; best in a well-drained soil in sun or partial shade	*N. × faassenii* 'Six Hills Giant'
Nerine bowdenii	half-hardy, bulbous plant with striking flowers in late summer and autumn	adds colour to the border in late summer	not fully hardy; requires well-drained soil in a sunny position	*N. bowdenii* 'Fenwick's Variety'
Nigella damascena (Love in a Mist)	interesting, hardy annual with attractive flower and fruit; blue or white flowers are produced on erect stems in summer	adds colour, form and texture to mixed borders in summer	requires well-prepared soil in full sun; dead-heading will improve flowering	*N. damascena*: 'Miss Jekyll Blue', 'Persian Jewels Mixed'
Oenothera biennis (Evening Primrose)	tall-growing, hardy biennial with pale yellow flowers in summer	adds height and colour to mixed border	best in an open, well-drained, sunny site	
Olearia macrodonta	potentially large, white-flowering, hardy, evergreen shrub with holly-like leaves which produce a musky odour	as large, structural plant and for summer flower interest	best in a sunny but protected position in well-drained loam	
Papaver nudicaule (Iceland Poppy)	truly a perennial but usually grown in Britain as a biennial or half-hardy annual; the white or yellow, fragrant flowers are carried on slender stems in summer	adds colour and texture to the border	requires well-drained soil in full sun	*P. nudicaule*: 'Champagne Bubbles', 'Kelmscott Strain'
Penstemon roezlii	low, spreading sub-shrub with blue flowers in July	for rock gardens and the front of borders	requires well-drained soil in full sun	
Perovskia atriplicifolia	tall, herbaceous plant with grey-green, aromatic leaves and violet-blue flowers in late summer	for colour and textural interest	requires sunny position in well-drained soil	*P. atriplicifolia*: 'Blue Mist', 'Blue Spire'

Plant Name	Description	Uses	Restrictions	Species/Varieties
Petunia × hybrida	large selection of half-hardy annuals with trumpet-shaped flowers	very popular plant for brightening the front of borders, for tubs and hanging baskets	requires shelter from cold winds in a well-drained, light soil	
Philadelphus coronarius (Mock Orange)	large, hardy, deciduous shrub with white, very fragrant flowers in midsummer	excellent shrub for semi-shaded bed or border and one of the best for drought conditions	best in well-drained soil	P. coronarius 'Aureus'
Phlomis fruticosa (Jerusalem Sage)	medium-sized, evergreen shrub with grey-green, woolly foliage and yellow flowers in summer	as intermediate planting for the mixed border in a sunny but protected position	requires well-drained soil in a sunny position	
Phlox drummondii	colourful, half-hardy annual which flowers July–September	good addition to the flower or shrub border	likes a well-drained soil in an open, sunny site	
Phormium tenax (New Zealand Flax)	interesting evergreen shrub which forms spikes of narrow leaves with tall flowers on mature plants	as architectural plant or small focal point	should be considered tender in some of the colder regions; requires a well-drained soil in full sun	P. tenax: 'Bronze Baby', 'Dazzler', 'Marie Sunrise', 'Purpureum', 'Sundowner', 'Tricolor', 'Yellow Wave'
Phygelius capensis	medium-height, red-flowering, evergreen shrub with a very open habit	may be trained as a wall shrub or grown in protected but sunny border	should not be considered hardy	P. capensis 'Coccineus'
Pinus (Pine)	large genus of evergreen, coniferous trees, some becoming extremely tall	as focal points; for form and textural interest especially in the low forms in rock gardens	care should be taken to select the correct size	

Plant	Description	Use	Conditions	Varieties
Piptanthus laburnifolius	low-growing, evergreen shrub with bright green, sweet-pea-like flowers in May	for colourful intermediate planting in the protected border	should not be considered hardy in any but the mildest regions	
Platanus × *hispanica* (London Plane)	very attractive, large, deciduous tree which is one of the most successful for general planting because it is resistant to pollution and easy to maintain	as large specimen or ornamental tree with attractively marked bark and Acer-like leaves	does not do well in shallow, alkaline soils	*P.* × *hispanica* 'Suttneri'
Platycodon grandiflorum (Balloon Flower)	hardy, herbaceous perennial with blue-green leaves and blue flowers in summer	for foliage and flower interest in sunny mixed border	prefers a well-drained soil	*P. grandiflorum*: 'Album', 'Mother of Pearl', 'Snowflakes'
Polygonum baldschuanicum (Russian Vine)	extremely quick and vigorous climber with white or pale pink flowers in summer	to cover old trees, trellises or fences quickly	take care where you plant this climber as, left unchecked, it will run rampant and can cause considerable damage to the supporting structure	
Portulaca grandiflora (Sun Plant)	low-growing, succulent with extremely colourful flowers	when carefully positioned will add colour to a bed or border	requires well-drained soil in full sun	*P. grandiflora*: 'Double Mixed', 'Single Mixed', 'Sunglo'
Potentilla fruticosa	summer-flowering, hardy, deciduous shrub	adds colour and texture to the mixed border	requires well-prepared soil in full sun or partial shade	*P. fruticosa*: 'Daydawn', 'Elizabeth', 'Golddigger', 'Goldfinger', 'Katherine Dykes', 'Klondike', 'Longacre', 'Primrose Beauty', 'Princess', 'Red Ace', 'Royal Flush', 'Sunset', 'Tangerine'
Populus alba (White Poplar)	potentially large, hardy, deciduous tree with silver-grey foliage and small, pale yellow catkins in spring	as large specimen tree or with others to form a windbreak; takes well to pollarding	best in full sun in a well-prepared, rich soil	

Plant Name	Description	Uses	Restrictions	Species/Varieties
Primula	hardy perennials with interesting foliage and colourful flowers; the plants listed here are all alpine primulas	adds bright colour to the rock garden or the front of a low border	requires rich but well-drained soil; leaves must be protected from water damage in winter	*P. allionii* *P. ameona* *P. auricula* *P. clarkei* *P. farinosa* *P. frondosa* *P. juliae* *P. marinata* *P. reidii*
Prunus laurocerasus (Common Laurel)	large, vigorous shrub with good foliage and white flowers in April	one of the best large structural shrubs; good for hedging or screening both in sun and shade; *P. laurocerasus* 'Otto Luyken' is a smaller shrub suitable for intermediate planting in large mixed borders	beware of damaging roots when working round this shrub	*P. laurocerasus* 'Otto Luyken'
Prunus lusitanica (Portugal Laurel)	large, vigorous shrub with glossy green foliage and creamy-white flowers in June	another excellent large structural shrub; good for hedging or screening	beware of damaging roots when working round this shrub	*P. lusitanica* 'Variegata'
Quercus rubra (Red Oak)	large, hardy, deciduous tree	the best oak for industrial planting and an excellent specimen tree when fully grown; good autumn colour	must have lime-free soil	
Rhus (Sumach)	attractive, hardy, deciduous shrub or small tree with wonderful autumn foliage colour and interesting bark	as small specimen tree or focal point; does well in polluted areas	sap may cause skin irritation; does best in sunny position in normal soil	*R. glabra* *R. trichocarpa* *R. typhina*

Name	Description	Use	Growing conditions	Cultivars/species
Robinia pseudoacacia (False Acacia)	most attractive, medium to large, deciduous tree with divided leaves similar to an ash	usually grown for its form and foliage; *R. pseudoacacia* 'Frisia' is one of the most suitable trees for a small garden	branches may be damaged by strong winds; best in a sunny but protected position	*R. pseudoacacia*: 'Bessoniana', 'Frisia', 'Inermis', 'Pyramidalis', 'Rozynskyana', 'Tortuosa'
Romneya (Tree Poppy)	interesting herbaceous perennial with poppy-like flowers	adds colour and form to the mixed border	should not be considered hardy in any but the mildest regions; must have extremely well-prepared soil with plenty of organic material	*R. coulteri* *R. trichocalyx* *R.* × *hybrida*
Rosmarinus officinalis (Rosemary)	small, aromatic, evergreen shrub with grey-green foliage and clusters of small, blue flowers in late spring	as culinary herb; as small shrub for the front of the border	does not like deep shade or alkaline soils	*R. officinalis*: 'Albus', 'Aurea Variegata', 'Benenden Blue', 'Fastigiatus', 'Jessop's Upright', 'Roseus', 'Tuscan Blue'
Rubbeckia laciniata (Cornflower)	extremely tall, yellow-flowering, herbaceous perennial	adds height to the border	requires well-drained soil in an open, sunny site	*R. laciniata*: 'Golden Glow', 'Goldquelle'
Rubus tridel (Benenden)	quick-growing, tall, deciduous shrub with interesting flower and foliage	for the mixed border and bright flower colour in early summer	does not do well in deep shade; requires well-drained soil	
Ruta graveolens (Rue)	low-growing, evergreen shrub with blue-grey foliage and small, deep yellow flowers in summer	for the front of the shrub or mixed border	foliage may be damaged by frost	
Salix alba (White Willow)	medium-sized, deciduous tree with attractive silver stems and foliage	as large focal point or specimen tree	best in full sun	

Plant Name	Description	Uses	Restrictions	Species/Varieties
Sambucus (Elder)	hardy, deciduous shrubs and small trees with interesting foliage, flower and fruit	good for informal or woodland planting; forms a fine, large, summer focal point when grown singly; berries are used for winemaking; very quick-growing when young	hardy down to –10°C	*S. canadensis* *S. nigra*
Santolina chamaecyparissus (Cotton Lavender)	low-growing, evergreen shrub with attractive, grey foliage and yellow flowers in midsummer	for massed planting in the front of the border; for large rock gardens; will form a low, informal hedge when planted 35–40cm apart	must have full sun and a well-drained soil	*S. neapolitana*
Scabiosa atropurpurea (Sweet Scabious)	tall-growing, hardy annual with deep crimson flowers in summer	adds height, form and colour to the mixed border	requires a rich but well-drained soil in a sunny position	*S. atropurpurea*: 'Bressingham White', 'Clive Greaves', 'Moonstone', 'Penhill Blue'
Sedum (Stonecrops)	large genus of hardy, evergreen, flowering plants with large heads of flowers that are extremely attractive to bees	for large rock gardens and for mass planting at the front of large mixed borders	requires well-drained soil in full sun	*S. acre* *S. aizoon* *S. album* *S. caeruleum* *S. cauticolum* *S. dasyphyllum* *S. ewersii* *S. floriferum* *S. spathulifolium* 'Capa Blanca' *S. spectabile* *S. spurium* *S. variegatum* *S.* × 'Autumn Joy' *S.* × Ruby Glow'

Sempervivum (Houseleek)	hardy, low-growing, rosette-forming succulents	for foliage and flower interest on rock gardens, dry walls and scree beds	requires well-drained soil in sun	*S. arachnoideum* *S. dolomiticum* *S. erythraeum* *S. heuffelii* *S. montanum* *S. soboliferum* *S. tectorum*
Senecio × 'Sunshine' (Greyi)	small, attractive, grey-leaved, evergreen shrub with bright yellow flowers in summer	the straggly habit of this plant makes it suitable for softening the harsh lines of paving where it abuts the border	should not be considered hardy in cold regions; requires a well-drained soil in sun or partial shade	
Sophora japonica (Japanese Pagoda Tree)	potentially very large hardy, deciduous shrub with creamy-white flowers in September followed by large pods in hot summers	good but informal specimen tree or fairly large focal point	requires a position in full sun but with shelter from cold winds; best in a rich but well-drained soil	
Sorbaria aitchisonii	large, hardy, deciduous shrub which bears large creamy-white flowers in summer	as large, quick-growing plant for the back of the shrub or mixed border	does not like deep shade; requires a well-drained soil	
Sorbus aria (Common Whitebeam)	medium, hardy, deciduous tree with interesting silver-white young foliage, creamy-white flowers, red berries and good autumn colour	as medium-sized specimen tree	best in full sun	*S. aria*: 'Chrysophylla', 'Lutescens', 'Majestica'
Spartium junceum (Spanish Broom)	large, hardy, deciduous shrub with golden-yellow, pea-like flowers in summer	for flower and foliage interest in an alkaline soil; good for coastal planting	requires an open, sunny position in a well-drained soil	

Plant Name	Description	Uses	Restrictions	Species/Varieties
Spiraea thunbergii	large, white-flowered, hardy deciduous shrub with arching branchlets and light green leaves	adds colour and texture to the border; will also form large, informal flowering hedge	requires well-prepared, deep rich soil in open sunny site	
Stephanandra incisa	large, hardy, deciduous, green-white flowering shrub	interesting addition to the large shrub border; good yellow foliage colour in autumn	does not like deep shade; requires a well-drained soil	S. incisa 'Prostrata'
Symphoracarpus (Snowberry)	hardy, deciduous shrub grown for its foliage and winter berries	adds colour to the winter border; also used in flower arranging	can be invasive	S. albus 'White Hedger' S. orbiculatus 'Variegatus' S. x doorenbosii
Syringa microphylla (Lilac)	small to medium-sized, hardy, deciduous shrub with large, fragrant, lilac-coloured flowers in June and again in September	adds colour to a border or large rock garden	does not like very alkaline soils or deep shade	S. microphylla 'Superba'
Tagetes erecta (Marigold)	tall-growing, half-hardy annual which bears lemon-yellow, daisy-like flowers in summer	excellent for the rich-coloured, mixed border and for cut flowers		T. patula
Tamarix pentandra (Five Stamen Tamarix)	large, deciduous shrub with interesting pink flowers	for interest in large shrub or mixed border	requires a well-drained soil	
Teucrium fruticans (Shrubby Germander)	medium to large, evergreen shrub with silver-grey foliage and small, light blue flowers in summer	for foliage and flower interest in a large, protected border, or fan-trained on a south-facing wall	must have a well-drained soil; only hardy down to −5°C	
Thymus vulgaris (Thyme)	hardy, aromatic, low-growing, evergreen, flowering shrub	for flower and foliage interest at the front of the border	requires a well-drained soil in full sun	

Name	Description	Use	Conditions	Species/Varieties
Tilia (Lime)	medium and large, hardy, deciduous trees with attractive foliage and form	as large focal point; tolerates polluted atmosphere	although *Tilia* are flowering trees, the flowers are inconspicuous	*T. cordata* *T. mongolica* *T. petiolaris* *T. platyphyllos* *T. tomentosa*
Tropaeolum majus	large, climbing, hardy annual with attractive yellow or orange trumpet-shaped flowers in summer	excellent for covering trellises, banks and unsightly fences	best in poor soil in a sunny position	*T. majus*: 'Alaska', 'Empress of India', 'Jewel Mixed', 'Scarlet Gleam', 'Whirlybird'
Tulipa (Tulip)	large genus of hardy bulbs	adds brilliant colour to the border in late spring	the larger, more ornamental bulbs are difficult to integrate informally; requires a well-drained soil in full sun	*T.*: 'Darwin Hybrid', 'Double Early', 'Greigii Hybrid', 'Kaufmanniana Hybrid'
Ulex europaeus (Gorse)	medium to large, hardy, evergreen shrub with rich yellow, pea-like flowers in spring	for flower colour and as structural plant	as this plant easily catches fire when dry, it should not be grown next to any buildings; requires a well-drained soil in full sun	*U. europaeus* 'Plenus'
Ursinia anethoides	medium-height, half-hardy perennial with large, daisy-like flowers in summer	as an annual for mixed borders and for cut flowers	requires a well-drained soil in full sun	*U. anethoides* 'Sunstar'
Veronica prostrata (Speedwell)	low-growing, deep-blue flowering, hardy perennial	for rock gardens and dry walls; for colour and texture in early summer; looks good against weathered rocks and is also an excellent summer ground cover plant	requires a well-drained soil in full sun	*V. prostrata*: 'Mrs Holt', 'Pygmaea', 'Rosea', 'Spode Blue'

Plant Name	Description	Uses	Restrictions	Species/Varieties
Viola odorata (Sweet Violet)	small, spreading, herbaceous perennial with delightful purple or white flowers in late winter and early spring	for ground cover and early flower colour		*V. odorata*: 'Christmas', 'Marie Louise', 'Princess of Wales', 'Sulphurea'
Vinca major (Greater Periwinkle)	arching, hardy evergreen, flowering shrub	as bold ground cover for large borders	does not grow well in heavy soils; best in light shade	*V. major*: 'Elegantissima', 'Maculata', 'Variegata'
Vinca minor (Lesser Periwinkle)	very low, evergreen, hardy, flowering shrub	as low ground cover for underplanting larger deciduous shrubs	does not grow well in heavy soils; best in light shade	*V. minor*: 'Alba', 'Albo Pleno', 'Atropurpurea', 'Aureo-variegata', 'Aureo-variegata Alba', 'Aureo Flore Pleno', 'Bowles Variety', 'Burgundy', 'Gertrude Jekyll', 'La Grave', 'Multiplex', 'Variegata'
Yucca	evergreen shrub with long, narrow leaves and large spikes of creamy-white flowers	one of the best architectural plants when fully grown	very slow to establish; requires full sun and well-drained soil	*Y. brevifolia* *Y. filamentosa* *Y. flaccida* 'Ivory' *Y. florida* 'Variegata' *Y. gloriosa* 'Variegata', *Y. recurvifolia* *Y. whipplei*
Zauschneria californica (Californian Fuchsia)	medium-height, tender perennial with grey-green leaves and bright red flowers in late summer and early autumn	for foliage interest and late 'hot' flower colour in mild regions of Britain	must not be considered hardy; requires a well-drained soil in full sun; best against a south-facing wall	*Z. californica* 'Dublin Variety'
Zinnia elegans	half-hardy annual growing to a height of 75cm with large, showy flowers	adds colour and height to a border; also very good as a cut flower	best in a rich but well-drained soil in a sunny, sheltered position	*Z. elegans*: 'Blaze', 'Burpee Hybrids', 'Envy', 'Fairyland', 'Peter Pan', 'Ruffles', 'State Fare', 'Super Giants'

Useful Addresses

The Countryside Commission,
John Dower House,
Crescent Place,
Cheltenham,
Gloucester GL50 3RA

English Nature,
Northminster House,
Peterborough,
Lincolnshire PE1 1UA

The Pesticides Trust,
23 Beehive Place,
London SW9 7QR

The Royal Society for the
Prevention of Cruelty to Animals,
The Causeway,
Horsham,
West Sussex RH12 1HG

The British Butterfly Conservation
Society,
Tudor House,
102 Chaveney Road,
Quorn,
Loughborough,
Leicestershire

The Urban Wildlife Trust,
The Jubilee Trades Centre,
130 Pershore Street,
Birmingham B5 6ND

The Royal Society for Nature
Conservation,
The Green,
Witham Park,
Waterside South,
Lincoln LN5 7JR

The Royal Society for the
Protection of Birds,
The Lodge,
Sandy,
Bedfordshire SG19 2DL

The Hardy Plant Society,
Bank Cottage,
Great Comberton,
Nr Pershore,
Worcestershire WR10 3DP

Soil Association,
86 Colston Street,
Bristol,
Avon BS1 5BB

Society of Garden Designers,
23 Reigate Road,
Ewell,
Surrey KT17 1PS

The Institute of Horticulture,
PO Box 313,
80 Vincent Square,
London SW1P 2PE

Index

Numbers in italics refer to line illustrations